IT'S A JUNGLE OUT THERE

MASCOT TALES
FROM TEXAS HIGH SCHOOLS

IT'S A JUNGLE OUT THERE

MASCOT TALES
FROM TEXAS HIGH SCHOOLS

Rob Sledge

State House Press

Press

McMurry University

Abilene, Texas

Library of Congress Cataloging-in-Publication Data

Sledge, Rob.
It's a jungle out there : mascot tales from Texas high schools / by
Rob Sledge.
    p. cm.
    Includes bibliographical references.
    ISBN-13: 978-1-880510-94-0 (pbk. : alk. paper)
    ISBN-10: 1-880510-94-4 (pbk. : alk. paper)
1. School mascots--Texas. 2. High schools--Texas. I. Title.

LB3633.S585 2005
371--dc22

        2005017449

State House Press
McMurry Station, Box 637
Abilene, TX 79697-0637
(325) 793-4682
www.mcwhiney.org

ISBN: 1-880510-94-4
10 9 8 7 6 5 4 3 2 1

Distributed by Texas A&M University Press Consortium
www.tamu.edu/upress
1-800-826-8911

Book Design by Rosenbohm Graphic Design

Dedicated to the memory of
BUDDY, a fallen Eagle

For future editions of this book, the reader is invited to send corrections, additions, and other suggestions to

Mascot Book
State House Press
Box 637, McMurry Station
Abilene, Texas 79697
or
rsledge@mcm.edu

In compiling this material, we probably got some of it wrong, and we were not able to do more than sample the schools of the state for stories. We especially would like to hear more stories about mascots past and present. The list of schools that follows omits several unusual institutions (magnet schools that don't have mascots, some private institutions, newly formed schools, others) but we think this list of more than 1,550 schools covers the state pretty well. We'd appreciate hearing from you if you were left out.

Contents

Introductions

The concept of having totems to identify your group traces back into the mists of antiquity. This practice is shown in the title of a recent book, *The Clan of the Cave Bear*, set 25,000 years ago. Roman legions carried silver eagles on a pole to lead the way into battle, a practice later emulated by Napoleon. A legion was forever disgraced if it lost its Eagle. Viking longships had carved beasts on their bows and Viking raiders carried specially decorated shields. In the middle ages, knights went forth emblazoned in heraldic designs, featuring dragons, unicorns, lions, and other ferocious beasts. In more recent times, flags have become the most visible symbols of group integrity and mutual support.

These symbols differentiated the in-group from the rest of the world and served as a rallying point in battle. In the American Civil War, the regimental standard bearers were the first targets of sharpshooters, and men would fight to the death to defend (or take) a regimental flag. Modern soldiers wear shoulder patches and paint national and squadron insignia on their airplanes.

People can get very emotional over symbols. Some symbols take on near-religious importance. There has been talk of a constitutional amendment banning the desecration of the American flag. There is controversy over the use of the Confederate battle flag in schools and public buildings. Flags are really only pieces of cloth, but there are those who will die to defend them—and what they represent. Some Native American groups passionately denounce the use of Indian mascots—while others defend the practice. Seldom is there a middle ground.

Texas high schools are no different. When their athletic teams (and academic teams) go forth to compete with other schools, they rally around their totem with cheers, fight songs, distinctive colors, chants, unique traditions, letter jackets, and costumed mascots. Though real critters were once used, the University Interscholastic League, which governs public high school programs in Texas, has banned the use of live animal mascots. Only stuffed beasts or costumed representations of the school symbol may now be displayed at competitions.

The schools and their fans take their mascots very seriously. But this book . . . well, IT doesn't do so because . . .

It's A Jungle Out There in Texas High Schools

Most Texans believe that it is safe to walk the highways and byways of the state. No recent Comanche raids have been reported, nor do wolves lurk to snatch up unguarded babies. There hasn't been a stagecoach holdup in years. John Wesley Hardin, Sam Bass, Black Jack Ketchum, Bonnie and Clyde, and their ilk have long since gone to their rewards (whatever they may be), Few Texans encounter rattlesnakes these days except at "rattlesnake roundups."

But be warned! Behind the doors of every high school in the state crouch vicious beasts and predators, ready, able, and even eager to pounce on the unsuspecting visitor. Texas may appear to be civilized, but . . . IT'S A JUNGLE OUT THERE.

There follows a guide to the perils that await the unwary in the Lone Star State. Take heed, lest you too fall victim to the denizens of this jungle.

Abilene Eagles

Junction Eagles

The Most Popular Mascot
THE EAGLE

The creature that one meets most frequently on safari through Texas shares the sky with a wide range of raptors. The fierce symbol of the United States is also the totem of many Texas schools . . . the **EAGLE**. It comes in several forms, including **Golden Eagles** (Klein Forest of Houston, for example), **War Eagles** (such as Oak Ridge of Conroe), and **Fighting Eagles** (like DeSoto's)—but beware—it COMES! One school, Destiny of San Antonio, even calls its teams **Willing Eagles** and **Lady Willing Eagles**. We're not quite sure what it is they are willing to do but it's probably not pleasant for their opponents.

MORE EAGLES THAN YOU CAN SHAKE A STICK AT

There are nearly 160 different schools with Eagle mascots, the largest number of any nickname. Ten percent of the state's schools are represented by EAGLES! And more are yet to come. Humble ISD doesn't plan to open Atascocita High School until 2006—but they are already named "Eagles." (See Appendix A for a complete list of Eagles.)

11

GOOD CHOICE #1
Guess what the Eagle Pass team nickname is.

COMPLETE AERIAL COVERAGE OF THE STATE

San Antonio
Brackenridge
Eagles

This ubiquitous raptor inhabits every corner of Texas, from Brownsville (Hanna) to El Paso (Andress), from Channing in the Northern Panhandle to Newton on the Louisiana border, to Detroit near the Oklahoma-Arkansas-Texas junction and all points in between.

HE DIDN'T HAVE THE HAT THEN
The great Tom Landry was a star for the Mission **Eagles**.

FAMOUS EAGLES
Dan Blocker, actor (Hoss Cartwright), O'Donnell, 1946
Bob Bullock, politician (Lt. Gov. of Texas), Hillsboro, 1947
Lyndon Johnson, politician (U.S. President), Johnson City, 1924
Anne Rice, writer (true mysteries), Richardson, 1959
Lloyd Bentsen, politician (U.S. Senator), Mission, 1939
Byron Hanspard, football player (Doak Walker Award, 1996), DeSoto
Trevor Cobb, football player (Doak Walker Award, 1991), Pasadena

12

MOST POPULAR TEAM NAMES

Texas High Schools	Rank	US Colleges
Eagles 159	1	Eagles
Bulldogs 97	2	Tigers
Tigers 78	3	Cougars
Lions 70	4	Bulldogs
Panthers 68	5	Warriors
Mustangs 61	6	Lions
Wildcats 56	7	Panthers
Cougars 45	8	Indians
Indians 37	9	Wildcats
Hornets 35	10	Bears
Warriors 33	11	
Pirates 33	12	
Bobcats 30	13	
Bears 28	14	
Knights 26	15	
Longhorns 25	16	
Yellowjackets 24	17	
Trojans 23	18	
Falcons 22	19	
Cardinals 21	20	
Raiders 20	21	
Owls 17	22	
Rams 16	23	
Cowboys 15	24	
Hawks 15	24	
Jaguars 15	24	

There are over 1,550 schools represented on our list and just over 10 per cent (159) of them are **Eagles**. Together, more than half the teams are named some form of **Eagles**, **Bulldogs**, **Tigers**, **Lions**, **Panthers**, **Mustangs**, **Wildcats**, **Cougars**, **Indians**, **Hornets**, **Pirates**, **Warriors**, or **Bobcats**—the first thirteen names on the list. Over 100 teams have names unique to themselves. (Note: This does not account for modifiers like "Fighting" or alternative spellings such as "Bobkatz.") Further, the list applies to boys teams only. Girls teams sometimes have different names. It should also be mentioned that we may well have missed counting some schools that are new or which have no athletic programs. Nevertheless, this list probably includes 99% of the high schools in the state, public and private.

Fort Worth
Country Day School
Falcons

Crane
Golden
Cranes

Gifted and Talonted

Look out below! Besides all those Eagles, the skies of Texas are also filled with other raptors—**Hawks** (Hardin-Jefferson, for example), **Falcons** (Midway of Henrietta), **Seahawks** (Riviera-Kaufer), and **Owls** (Hondo, Garland, Odem are a few). To add injury to injury, the teams from Joshua and Reagan County of Big Lake are the *Fighting* **Owls**.

BIRDS OF A FEATHER FLOCK TOGETHER

In this case, it's **Falcons** to the Houston area. Ten of the twenty-two Falcon schools in the state are there, including Jones (Houston), Jersey Village (Houston), Kinkaid (Houston), Hargrave (Huffman), Incarnate Word (Houston), Foster (Richmond), Royal (Brookshire), Clear Lake (Houston), Southeast Academy (Houston) and Channelview. Another flock nests in the Metroplex—Bishop Dunne (Dallas), Country Day School (Fort Worth), Fairhill School (Dallas), Fulton Academy (Heath), Lake Dallas, A. Maceo Smith (Dallas) and Metro Opportunity School (Fort Worth). The other five Falcon schools are scattered around the rest of the state.

WHOOOOOO ?

Hale Center, San Antonio Highlands, Anderson, Chireno, that's who. They're all **Owls**.

GOOD CHOICE #2
Hawkins, as you might expect, is the **Hawks**!

TOUGH OL' BIRDS
There are other birds of less fearsome reputation, but of equal potential for mischief among the unsuspecting. For example, there are some pretty rough **Parrots** (Fort Worth Polytechnic), **Ducks** (Taylor), **Bluejays** (Snook and Needville), and **Cardinals** (Bridge City, Del Valle, Maud, among others) out there. Alfred Hitchcock, take note!

Fort Worth
Polytechnic
Parrots

We also have **Skylarks** (the girls of St. Francis Academy in San Antonio) and **Chaparrals** (Austin Westlake is a very successful example). Don't look for Chaparrals in the sky; though they can fly after a fashion, they're usually called **Roadrunners** (such as Waldorf School in Austin).

EVERYTHING IS JUST DUCKY IN TAYLOR
Taylor adopted the **Duck** mascot in 1924, a wet year in central Texas. The football team played enough games in the mud that season to make people remark that they were just like a flock of ducks. And the coach's name was C.R. Drake, so "Drake's Ducks" was a logical result. The football field became known henceforth as the "Duck Pond."

Taylor
Ducks

POLY WANTS A VICTIM
Fort Worth Polytechnic High School got the nickname "**Parrots**" because its real name was usually shortened to "Poly;" hence, Poly Parrots.

GOOD CHOICE #3
Crane's teams are the **Golden Cranes.**

THE FIRST LADIES OF TEXAS

Jayton is the home of the appropriately named **Jaybirds**. But it was not always so. Jayton started off as "Daredevils," then dropped football and didn't have a mascot. In 1935 they adopted black and gold as school colors and became "Black Kats" for non-football squads; when football came back, somebody, perhaps the local paper, called them the Jaybirds. Jayton may have been the first to have "Lady" attached to the girls' teams.

Jayton
Jaybirds

THEY RAISE A LOT OF RICE AROUND EL CAMPO, IN CASE YOU WERE WONDERING.

For those who fancy a more exotic species, you can find the **Rice-birds** at El Campo (if they don't find you first.)

STATE BIRDS—THEIRS, NOT OURS

Surprisingly, no one has adopted the Texas state bird—there are no Mockingbirds on the list. But there is a tough nest of **Yellowhammers** at Rotan. That's the state bird of Alabama. And all those **Cardinals** (Columbus, Harlingen, High Island, MacArthur of Irving, Southside of San Antonio, among others) represent the state bird of Virginia, West Virginia, Ohio, North Carolina, Illinois, Indiana, and Kentucky.

Irving
Cardinals

Austin
Westlake
Chaparrals

Plus—the Roadrunner (a.k.a. **Chaparrals,** as in Fort Worth Wyatt, Aubrey) is the state bird of New Mexico.

YELLOWHAMMERS = ORANGE WOODPECKERS

Rotan was named **Yellowhammers** after a woodpecker supposedly found in South Texas; the name was chosen by student vote. At first, though, not everyone knew that a yellowhammer was a bird; somebody sewed a set of jerseys embroidered with a hammer. That had to be changed. It's not a hammer nor is it yellow—the school colors are orange and white!

IT CAN'T HURT THAT THEY'RE
FROM BIRDVILLE, EITHER

Birdville **Hawks** are named after two red-tailed hawks that nested near the school.

WHAT A SURPRISE!

Nobody (so far) has opted for Vultures or Buzzards as their school mascots.

BENJAMIN FRANKLIN WOULD BE PROUD
(OR WOULD HE?)

When the young United States was choosing symbols, Franklin suggested that the Turkey should be the national bird—crafty, wily, independent, self-sufficient. Franklin objected to the eagle because it was a bird of prey, a connotation he thought inappropriate. Well, you have seen what happened to that idea in Texas.

San Antonio Highlands Owls

But Franklin could have one consolation. One of the best nicknames in the state is that adopted by Cuero—the **Gobblers**. They used to call their junior high teams Turklets and the lower grades were Eggshells. Nowadays they are all Fighting Gobblers. By contrast, Valley High School in Turkey, Texas, calls its teams **Patriots**.

Cuero Gobblers

FAMOUS FALCONS

George W. Bush, politician (Gov. of Texas, U.S. president), Houston Kincaid

FAMOUS CHAPARRALS

Drew Brees, football player (Maxwell Trophy, 2000), Austin Westlake

17

FAMOUS CARDINALS

Dennis Quaid, actor, Houston Bellaire, 1972
Randy Quaid, actor, Houston Bellaire, 1968

FAMOUS DUCKS

Elmore "Rip" Torn, actor, Taylor

Menard
Yellowjackets

Mesquite
Skeeters

Bug Infestation

Even if you escape the birds, the insect life of Texas swarms with malevolent beasties—**Skeeters** (Mesquite), **Bumblebees** (Academy at Little River) and **Hornets** (the tenth most popular name, with Lometa, Flour Bluff, Holland, Muenster, Tulia, among others. See Appendix A). There seem to be **Yellowjackets** everywhere. (It's the seventeenth most popular name, including Fort Worth Arlington Heights, Alvin, Kermit, Meridian, Stephenville. See Appendix A). And that's just in the sky. Masonic Home of Fort Worth has **Mighty Mites** and Progreso has **Red Ants**.

WHAT? NO WASPS?

No school has Wasps for a mascot. And, though lots of teams are called "Indians" and "Vikings," there are no "WASPs" either. Maybe the Sweetwater girls should adopt that name. During World War II, Sweetwater was the national training base for the Women's Army Service Pilots—the WASPs.

BUGS OF A FEATHER FLOCK TOGETHER.

While a few larger schools have opted to be Hornets, the name is especially popular among the smaller schools. Of the 35 public school teams called **Hornets**, 21 belong to Class A, the smallest of the five classifications in the state, and eight of those are so small that they play six-man football. The only Hornet schools in the largest class are East Central (San Antonio) and Huntsville. Only one private school, Greenhill of Addison, has chosen to call its teams Hornets.

NO HIGH SCHOOL HAS HONORED THESE NASTIES . . . YET.

Edcouch-Elsa
Yellowjackets

At least three migratory bugs have wrought havoc in the state. Two of the pests came north from Mexico. They were the Cotton Boll Weevil in the 1890s and, nearly a century later, Fire Ants (pronounced "far aints," which arrived from South America via Mobile, Alabama) and Africanized Killer Bees. No high school has honored these little monsters with a team name (but see Robstown Junior High below), though we did have some state legislators called the "Killer Bees" a few years back. And there's an unofficial nest of them playing for the Houston Astros.

Aspermont
Hornets

NOT, AS THEY HASTEN TO ADD, THE STINKERS

In Aspermont, where the senior high teams are Hornets, the junior high nickname is the **Stingers**.

THEY BOTH MAKE THEIR LIVING OFF OF COTTON

The Robstown Junior High teams are **Weevils**. (The senior high team is **Cottonpickers**.)

IS SOMEBODY MISSING SOMETHING HERE?

Of the more than two dozen schools calling themselves *Yellow*jackets, only Arlington Heights of Fort Worth has *yellow* as one of the school colors. For the rest, the closest they get is gold or orange.

FAMOUS YELLOWJACKETS

Janis Joplin, singer, Port Arthur, 1960
John Denver, singer, Fort Worth Arlington Heights, 1961
Jimmy Johnson, football coach, Port Arthur, 1961
Nolan Ryan, baseball player, Alvin, 1965
Phyllis George, journalist (Miss America, 1971), Denison, 1967

FAMOUS HORNETS

Lou Diamond Phillips, actor, Flour Bluff
Billy Sims, football player (Heisman Trophy, 1975), Hooks

20

MOVIE MATCHUPS

Which movies come to mind when you consider the possible confrontations below?

A. Lifestyle Christian of Conroe Victors vs. Victoria Memorial Vipers

B. Houston Lee Generals vs. Dallas Kimball Knights

C. Grapeland Sandies vs. Port Lavaca Sandcrabs

D. Brownwood Lions at Winters Blizzards

E. Lamesa Tornadoes vs. Hightower (Missouri City) Hurricanes

F. Celeste Blue Devils vs. Needville Bluejays

G. Gonzales Apaches vs. Richmond Bush Broncos

H. Midland Lee Rebels with an open date

I. Santa Anna Mountaineers vs. Wimberley Texans

J. Dallas Jefferson Patriots vs. Garland's Lakeview Centennial Patriots play
a doubleheader

(1) THE LIONS IN WINTERS   ____

(2) THE ALAMO   ____

(3) GONE WITH THE WIND   ____

(4) REBEL WITHOUT A CAUSE   ____

(5) THE BLUES BROTHERS   ____

(6) FORT APACHE, THE BRONX   ____

(7) AN OFFICER AND A GENTLEMAN   ____

(8) VICTOR/VICTORIA   ____

(9) PATRIOT GAMES   ____

(10) TRUE GRIT   ____

Clint Horizon
Scorpions

Tolar
Rattlers

Poisonous

Don't just keep looking up—you have to watch where you step, too. No, no, no—not just because of the Longhorns. When you walk the prairies or brush country, you should watch and listen for **Rattlers** (such as Rio Grande City, San Marcos, and San Antonio Reagan). And around Vanderbilt, somebody let **Cobras** loose. (Both Cobras and Brahmas are imports from India. You *really* have to watch where you put your feet there.) Those Cobras have recently spread to San Antonio Keystone, so they are multiplying. Victoria Memorial has a nest of **Vipers**.

No Texas high school teams are Copperheads, Moccasins, Coral Snakes, Spiders, or Vinegaroons, though all of these are found in the state. Perhaps they are just a little too nasty-tempered. On the other hand, don't relax too much—Fort Worth South Hills and Clint Horizon have some really wicked **Scorpions**.

NO KIDDING—POISONOUS FROGS

Not many people know this, but a type of indigenous toad (Bufo marinus) secretes a mild poison too, and there are **Bullfrogs** at Lake Worth. Lake Worth became Bullfrogs because of the inhabitants of a nearby creek.

CUTE AS A BUTTON !

San Antonio Central Catholic has teams called the **Buttons**. Central Catholic is a feeder school for St. Mary's University, which is Rattlers. Buttons are baby rattlesnakes.

SSSSSO SSSSSORRY, THE ADMINISSSSSTRATION SSSSSAYSSSSS NO RECOUNTSSSSS.

A few years ago, Victoria High School (Stingarees) merged with Stroman High School (Raiders) to form a new campus in Victoria called Memorial High School. According to one story, the student vote should have named the school Patriots, but someone in the administration allegedly stuffed the ballot box and the result was **Vipers**. It is hard, they say, to find a mascot costume shaped like a snake, or a student who can fit into it.

San Antonio
Ronald Reagan
Rattlers

GOOD CHOICE #4

The **Rattlers** of San Antonio Ronald Reagan High School have a booster club called the "Diamondbackers."

23

Richardson
Berkner
Rams

Burleson
Elks

Sharp Points

In Texas, horns or thorns or spines can be found everywhere.

There is no team (yet) named the Grassburrs, the Prickly Pears, the Mesquites, or the Palm Thorns, and Chaparral usually refers to the bird, not the thorny underbrush. The present author has had unpleasant encounters with all of those. But there *are* some **Burrs** at Chinquapin School near Houston.

Some teams are simply named for their horns—Kerrville's **Antlers**, the New Braunfels **Unicorns**, numerous **Longhorns**, and a few **Shorthorns** (Schulenburg and Marfa). Would you rather be impaled by an Antler or a Longhorn?

Other critters that sprout these dangerous weapons include **Bucks** (White Deer), **Antelope** (Abernathy, Whiteface), **Deer** (Deer Park, and Comfort's girls teams) and **Elks** (Evant, Stratford).

Separating the sheep from the goats could be a hazardous job if they include **Rams** (Del Rio, Mineral Wells, Alief Elsik, Allen Academy, El Paso Montwood) and **Goats** (Groesbeck) or **Angoras** (Rocksprings).

Stratford
Elks

IF YOU INSIST ON BEING TECHNICAL ABOUT IT, THEY'RE NOT REALLY FROGS—THEY'RE LIZARDS

So far no Texas high school has followed the lead of Texas Christian University by naming a team Horned Frogs. Yes, it's true—even the frogs have horns in Texas.

DON'T EVER GET STUCK IN SPRINGTOWN

The Springtown teams are **Porcupines.** In the mid-1920s, Springtown practiced and played basketball on an outdoor court. (So did many other schools, when gymnasiums were a luxury. Brownsville played outdoors until after World War II, but Brownsville is a lot farther south.) One day, the Springtown basketball coach suggested to the team that they go into a classroom and choose a mascot. Several suggestions came from the players, but they finally settled on a Porcupine because "no one wants to get near a porcupine, because they don't want quills in them." Much later, in the mid-

White Deer
Bucks

1980s, a coach suggested a battle cry of "Pojo!" It is possible they were just porcupining Odessa Permian's famous "Mojo." Anyway, the term is considered magic in Springtown today.

THEY CHOSE "RAMS" AS A LAST RESORT

Mineral Wells teams began as the Resorters. Mineral Wells, as the name suggests, was the home of springs that gushed forth what the locals called "Crazy Water," which attracted tourists to the resorts that grew up at the spa. Later, when that trade died down, they were called the Mountaineers. Yes, there are some hills nearby. More prosaically, they are now called the **Rams**. The women's teams are **Lady Rams**. The dictionary defines "ram" as a male sheep. So these are female male sheep?

DON'T LET THEM GET *YOUR* GOAT

Groesbeck may be **Goats** because of alliteration, but another explanation points to the "goathead" thorns that littered the early playing fields. The school formally chose the name in the 1920s, but it may have been around before then.

Rocksprings, in the heart of sheep and goat country, calls its high school teams **Angoras** and its junior high teams the **Billies**, which they take to mean "little goats." (In which case, "Billy the Kid" would be redundant, wouldn't it? Speaking of whom, there's a statue of him on the

Fredericksburg
Battlin' Billies

25

main street in Hico, where a man named "Brushy Bill" claimed to be the Kid years after Pat Garrett supposedly shot him in New Mexico.)

IT'S TRUE THEY'RE FROM THE HILL COUNTRY, BUT . . .

Fredericksburg's **Battlin' Billies** are billygoats, not hillbillies. However, one story says they really may have started out as "Hillbillies." Chester Nimitz left Fredericksburg for the Naval Academy, probably before the teams had names. He went on to command the U.S Pacific Fleet in World War II as a five-star admiral—a Hill Country boy in the Navy!

ANTELOPES

Post
Antelopes

The only three schools that have an **Antelope** for a mascot are fairly close together on the South Plains. According to the story told at Post, a bunch of guys sitting around the barber shop selected the nickname for the high school team—the Bold Gold Antelopes.

The town of Antelope, in Jack County, doesn't have a high school. Those kids go to Jacksboro and therefore become Tigers. Maybe this is where the mysterious "Jackalopes" come from?

FAMOUS ELKS

Kelly Clarkson, singer, Burleson, 2000

FAMOUS GOATS

Joe Don Baker, actor, Groesbeck

SPOTLIGHTING DEER

Chelsi Smith, Miss Universe, 1995, Deer Park
Andy Pettitte, baseball player, Deer Park, 1990

FAMOUS RAMS

Shelley Duvall, actress, Houston Waltrip, 1967
Patrick Swayze, actor, Houston Waltrip, 1971

MORE MOVIE MATCHUPS

Here's another set of contests that might have inspired motion picture titles.

A. Round Rock Stony Point Tigers vs. Round Rock High Dragons

B. Houston Sharpstown Apollos with too many men on the football field

C. Tyler Lee Red Raiders vs. Gladewater Sabine Cardinals

D. Atlanta Rabbits vs. Clyde Bulldogs

E. Whitehouse Wildcats with an open date

F. Graham Lady Blues vs. Farwell Lady Blues

G. Hardin Hornets vs. Academy Bumblebees

H. Breckinridge Buckaroos play Corpus Christi Miller Buccaneers

I. Seguin Matadors vs. Laredo Cigarroa Toros

J. Carrolton American Heritage Stars vs. Star Tigers

(1) THE STING   ____

(2) LADY SINGS THE BLUES   ____

(3) STAR WARS   ____

(4) CASABLANCA   ____

(5) APOLLO THIRTEEN   ____

(6) UNCLE BUCK   ____

(7) CROUCHING TIGER, HIDDEN DRAGON   ____

(8) RAGING BULL   ____

(9) REDS   ____

(10) BUNNIE AND CLYDE   ____

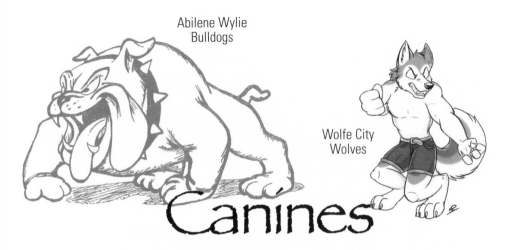

Abilene Wylie
Bulldogs

Wolfe City
Wolves

Canines

Once you get past the **Bulldogs** (IF you get past the **Bulldogs**) there aren't many dogs around . . . just a few **Greyhounds** (including San Benito, Boerne, Gruver, Taft, and Knox City, among others), **Huskies** (Captain Chapin of El Paso and Wichita Falls Hirschi), and one pack of **Bloodhounds** (Brownsville St. Joseph Academy).

They used to say Texas was heaven for men and horses and hell for women and dogs. Maybe so, but there's sure a lot of women in the state and there are nearly a hundred teams called Bulldogs, the second most prevalent nickname. These include Amherst, Sugarland Austin, Carthage, Jefferson, McAllen, Midland, North Zulch, Houston Reagan, Abilene Wylie, Clyde, and many others. (See Appendix A.) A recent addition to the kennel is the school that calls its teams **Bull-dawgs** (Bending Oaks of Dallas).

When you count **Wolves** (there are packs in Colorado City, Dilley, San Augustine, and Dalhart), **Gray Wolves** (Killeen Shoemaker), **Timber-wolves** (Cedar Park), **Lobos** (Levelland, Longview, etc.), and **Coyotes** (including Wichita Falls, Alice, Uvalde, and Borden County of Gail) in the canine realm, then the picture looks a little different. These predators are native to the state and they show up in lots of high schools. More distantly related are the **Foxes**, which may be found at Caddo Mills and, in their silver variety, at El Paso Jefferson. The **Swifts** of Nazareth, which sound like they might be birds, are really named for the "Swift Foxes" of the Texas Panhandle.

28

IN CENTRAL TEXAS, CEDAR DEFINITELY COUNTS AS "TIMBER."

Newcomers to the pack are the **Timberwolves** of Cedar Park. You can understand Dallas Spruce being Timberwolves, even if the only spruce trees in Big D are ornamentals. But what happened at Mansfield Timberview? They opted to be just plain **Wolves** instead of Timberwolves.

Cedar Park
Timberwolves

GOOD CHOICE #5

Wolfe City High is, naturally enough, the **Wolves**.

IT'S TRUE THAT COYOTES ARE MEANER THAN JERSEYS—USUALLY

Gail, boasting the only high school in Borden County, is named for Gail Borden, the founder of Borden milk company. So why are they **Coyotes**? Elsie, Borden's trademark critter, is a Jersey cow.

YOU MIGHT SAY HE GOT OFF TO A GOOD START

San Benito
Greyhounds

Bobby Morrow, the 1956 Olympic triple gold-medalist in the sprints, was a San Benito **Greyhound** in high school two years earlier.

IS ELVIS IN THE STADIUM?

Shouldn't Brownsville's St. Joseph **Bloodhounds** have "You Ain't Nothin' But a Houn' Dog" for its fight song?

IT CARRIED OVER INTO HIS REPORTING STYLE

Dan Rather played end for the Houston Reagan **Bulldog** football team in 1948.

WHAT'S UP, DOG?

Tex Avery, the cartoonist who created Bugs Bunny, was a graduate of North Dallas High (and therefore a **Bulldog**). The story around the school is that the rabbit's trademark phrase "What's up, doc?" was a byword in the halls of North Dallas long before Avery took it to Hollywood.

29

REAL LOBOS ARE SCARY!

Houston
Chávez Lobos

In the summer of 1925, an aspiring high school football player named LeRoy Murrah was dispatched to drive a tractor from his home in Levelland to Bledsoe forty miles to the west. Nightfall caught the slow-moving tractor out in the country. Murrah spent a restless night sitting on top of the tractor, listening nervously to wolves howling in the nearby sandhills. When school started that fall, and Levelland decided to designate a mascot for the school, young Murrah suggested **Lobos**, to commemorate his night on the tractor.

FAMOUS BULLDOGS

Mary Kay Wagner Ash, businesswoman, Houston Reagan, 1935
Jim Reeves, singer, Carthage, 1941
Jimmy Dean, singer, businessman, Plainview
Scott Appleton, football player (Outland Trophy, 1963), Brady
Sissy Spacek, actress, Quitman, 1968

FAMOUS WOLVES

Don Maynard, football player, Colorado City

FAMOUS GREYHOUNDS

Baldemar Huerta (Freddy Fender), singer, San Benito
Bob Lilly, football player, Throckmorton

Abilene Christian
Panthers

Texas (Texarkana) Tigers

Felines

While the state boasts a respectable collection of dogs, cats are a different situation. There's lots and lots of them in multiple varieties. We have **Blackcats** (Bay City and Mexia) and **Bluecats** (Coleman); **Bobcats** (Cy-Fair of Cypress, Edinburg, South San Antonio, among others) and **Tomcats** (Tom Bean); **Bearcats** (Ballinger, Sherman, Aledo) and **Bearkats** (Garden City and Raymondville).

Bearcat is an old name for Mountain Lion. Speaking of which, other Texas names given to that same critter are **Cougars** (Abilene Cooper, Jarrell, Houston Nimitz, The Colony) and **Jaguars** (Flower Mound, Austin LBJ, Houston Forest Brook). Though **Panthers** (Odessa Permian, North Lamar of Paris, Duncanville, Lufkin, Pflugerville, Weslaco) and **Leopards** (Dallas Adamson, Lorena, LaGrange) are a different breed of cat, some of them may really be mountain lions in disguise.

Ozona Lions

Often, feline predators are called just plain **Lions.** Most of the Texas Lions represent the African variety (Brownwood, Henderson, Lutheran of Dallas, Waco, Vernon). There's even a Texas Lions Camp—but it belongs to the civic club. One sophisticated group (Kingsville Academy) is known as the **Pride of Lions**. If grown Lions intimidate you, perhaps you could play with the

Brenham Cubs

Brenham **Cubs** (lion cubs, that is), but those Cubs play rough, so be prepared. The **Monarchs** of Poolville boast a lion logo—the "monarchs of the jungle." (Told you it's a jungle out there!)

Then we have **Lynxes** (Spearman) plus **Tigers** (A&M Consolidated, Dripping Springs, Slaton, Corsicana, San Isidro) galore. In fact, there are more of these carnivores than there is prey to feed them, unless a few tourists come along, of course—they looooove tourists. Like we said, it's a jungle out there and only the fittest survive. The most dangerous of all may be the mysterious **Wampus Cats** (at Itasca), pictured on the front cover of this book. (See box at the end of the chapter.)

HERE A CAT, THERE A CAT, EVERYWHERE A KITTY CAT

Almost a fourth (24 per cent) of the Texas mascots are some form of cat. **Tigers** are the third most prevalent (such as Lancaster, Mercedes, Mount Pleasant, Belton, Star), **Lions** fourth (including Calvary Academy of Denton, Granger, Livingston, New Boston, Pope John XXIII of Katy, Tyler John Tyler, Houston Yates, Sunnybrook Christian of San Antonio), **Panthers** fifth (Abilene Christian, Houston Jeff Davis, Klein Oak of Spring, Paradise, El Paso Austin), **Wildcats** seventh (Dallas Lake Highlands, Anthony, Palestine, Plano, Austin's Texas School for the Blind, Dallas Woodrow Wilson, Houston Wheatley), **Cougars** eighth (like Richardson Canyon Creek Christian, Buna, Katy Cinco Ranch, Santa Maria, Waco's Reicher Catholic), and **Bobcats** thirteenth (Blum, Kerens, New Braunfels Christian, Rio Hondo). Five of the top eight mascots are some form of feline. (See Appendix A for the full lists.)

Corpus Christi
Carroll Tigers

Plano Senior High
Wildcats

THEY AIN'T LYIN'

Panther Creek High School of Valera is the **Panthers** sure enough, but Leon of Jewett is not the Lions and DeLeon's mascot is the **Bearcat**—close, but not close enough.

COINCIDENCE? PROBABLY ... BUT STILL ...

The famous "Flying Tigers" of World War II were led by Maj. Gen. Claire Chennault, a native of Commerce, Texas. The mascot of Commerce is **Tigers**.

THAT'S THREE LIVES SO FAR—ONLY SIX MORE TO GO

Coleman started as "the Blue and White," then became the Blue Cats after a Russian Blue Cat, a popular animal in the 1920s. Somewhere along the way, that became one word.

Coleman Bluecats

CHRISTIANS AND LIONS

St. Mark's School of Dallas has a **Lion** mascot, which is appropriate because the usual Christian symbol for the gospel writer Mark is a lion. In fact, church schools seem to have an affinity for **Lions.** No less than twenty-three religious schools claim the beast as their mascot. (See Appendix A.)

WHETHER BOBCAT OR PUMA, A LION IS STILL A CLOSE RELATIVE

While Texas was still part of Mexico, a group of German farmers, including the von Roeder and Kleberg clans, settled in Austin's colony. One of the von Roeder sons shot a cat near a spring in what is now Austin County. The families built their village near the site, naming it Katzenquelle, or Cat Spring. One account says that the victim was a bobcat, while another holds that it was a puma. If you live in Cat Spring, Texas, today, you go to school in Sealy, where the mascot is the **Lion**.

Abilene Cooper
Cougars

WHAT DO YOU GET WHEN YOU CROSS A HORNET AND A BRONCO?

A merger of Mobeetie (Hornets) and Briscoe (Broncos) about twenty years ago created the Fort Elliott ISD. The merged school became the **Cougars**. In 2003, a third school was added to the district, when

33

the Cougars "ate up" the Allison Antelopes, incorporating those students as well.

MÁS GATOS

Edinburg, after many years with only one high school (the **Bobcats**), expanded to three schools. Economedes High School became the **Jaguars** and Edinburg North became the **Cougars**. The three schools share a football stadium called "Cat Memorial Stadium."

NOT YOUR ORDINARY TABBY

Actress Renee Zellweger ("Cold Mountain") must have been a real Tiger, according to one biographical website. At Katy High School, she was a gymnast, cheerleader, and member of the pep squad called the Bengal Brigade. In junior high, the site suggests, she enjoyed "joining in with boys in soccer, basketball, baseball, and even football."

DOUBLE GOOD CHOICE

The most famous softball player in Texas is Olympian Cat Osterman of the University of Texas and Cypress Springs High School. Naturally, the Cypress Springs mascot is a cat—a **Panther**! Her given name is Catherine, but almost nobody knows it—to the world, she's just CAT.

FAMOUS TIGERS

John Connally, politician (Gov. of Texas), Floresville, 1933
Guy Lewis, basketball coach, Arp, 1940
H. Ross Perot, businessman, politician, Texarkana, 1947
Don Meredith, football player, broadcasting, Mount Vernon, 1956
Jeannie C. Riley, singer, Anson, 1964
Roger Clemens, baseball player, Spring Woods, 1979
Eric Dickerson, football player, Sealy
Teresa Weatherspoon, basketball player, West Sabine, 1984
Horton Foote, writer (Pulitzer, two Oscars), Wharton, 1932

FAMOUS LIONS

Leon Jaworski, Watergate prosecutor, Waco, 1920
Jo-Carroll Dennison, Miss America, Tyler John Tyler, 1942
Dorothy Ann Willis (Ann Richards), politician (Gov. of Texas),
Waco, 1951
Boz Skaggs, singer, Dallas St. Mark's
Tommy Lee Jones, actor, Dallas St. Mark's, 1974
Earl Campbell, football player (Heisman Trophy, 1977)
Tyler John Tyler, 1974
Robert Van Winkle (Vanilla Ice), singer, Carrolton Turner

FAMOUS WILDCATS

Davey O'Brien, football player (Heisman Trophy, 1938),
Dallas Woodrow Wilson, 1935
Larry McMurtry, author, Archer City, 1954
Roy Orbison, singer, Wink, 1954
Waylon Jennings, singer, Littlefield
Forrest Gregg, football player, coach, Sulphur Springs, 1952
Lance Armstrong, cyclist, Plano East
Tim Brown, football player (Heisman Trophy, 1987),
Dallas Woodrow Wilson, 1984
Patsy McClenny (Morgan Fairchild), actress, Richardson
Lake Highlands, 1968
Justin Leonard, golfer, Richardson Lake Highlands, 1990
Barbara Jordan, politician (U.S. House of Representatives),
Houston Wheatley, 1952

FAMOUS COUGARS

Bob Estes, golfer, Abilene Cooper
Sam Adams, football player, Cypress Creek
Charles ("Bubba") Smith, football player, Beaumont
Charlton-Pollard, 1963
Kay Bailey Hutchinson, politician (U.S. Senate), La Marque, 1962

FAMOUS PANTHERS
Sandra Day O'Connor, jurist (U.S. Supreme Court),
El Paso Austin, 1946
Willie Nelson, singer, Abbott, 1951
Jerry LeVias, football player, Beaumont Hebert, 1965
Greg Ostertag, basketball player, Duncanville
Tamika Catchings, basketball player, Duncanville
Alan Bean, astronaut, Fort Worth Paschal, 1956
Kenny Rogers, singer, actor, Houston Jeff Davis, 1956
Harlon H. Block, war hero, Weslaco, 1943
(the kneeling Marine in the Iwo Jima flag-raising photo)

FAMOUS LEOPARDS
Ray Price, singer, Dallas Adamson, 1946
Michael Martin Murphey, singer, Dallas Adamson, 1963

FAMOUS BOBCATS
Fess Parker, actor, San Angelo Central, 1942

FAMOUS BEARKATS
Lyle Lovett, singer, Klein, 1975

FAMOUS BLACKCATS
Vickie Hogan (Anna Nicole Smith), entertainer, Mexia

THE TALE OF THE WAMPUS CAT

This mysterious creature originated as a legend among the Cherokee Indians of the southern Appalachians. It supposedly had large eyes, huge feet, and could walk on its hind legs—an evil forest spirit. Or maybe it was a human being that turned into a cat at night—a feline werewolf. Whatever it was, it was something to be feared.

In the early 1920s, about the time many Texas high schools were adopting their first mascots, Itasca chose the **Wampus Cat** to be its totem animal. One story from the school attributes the origin to the head cheerleader, who, after listening to the football team boast about the last game, blurted out "My, what a wampus cat!" She meant to agree that they had indeed fought ferociously. Another story holds that, after a particularly hard-won victory, one of the football players erupted with "Wow! We really played like Wampus Cats tonight!" and the nickname was born. A high school in Arkansas features the only other known appearance of this mythical creature.

Over the years, there have been many pictorial and costumed manifestations of the beast at Itasca High but, since no one can credibly claim to have seen one, any among them could be correct.

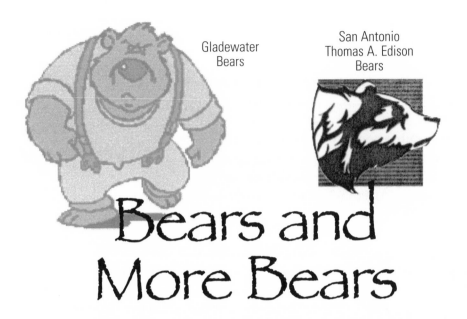

Gladewater
Bears

San Antonio
Thomas A. Edison
Bears

Bears and More Bears

Though Teddy Roosevelt recruited his "Rough Riders" in San Antonio, the "teddy bear" named for him came from another state. None of the Texas types is nearly so cuddly; Texas bears come equipped with claws and jaws. There are the Hastings (Alief) **Fighting Bears** and the South Oak Cliff (Dallas) **Golden Bears** and the Little Cypress-Mauriceville **Battlin' Bears**. You can find lots of others who are just plain **Bears** (Balmorhea, Gladewater, El Paso Bowie, Fort Worth Brewer, et al.), but don't tell them they're "just plain" without an escape route handy.

For alliteration, we have the Baird **Bears**. For appropriate names, there are the West Oso **Bears** ("Oso" is Spanish for "bear") and the Ursuline Academy (Dallas) **Bears** ("Ursa" is Latin for, what else, "bear"). The Ursuline campus store is called Bear Necessities. For yet more variety, there's the West Brook (Beaumont) **Bruins**. Lots of Bears! Come on around and let 'em give you a BIG HUG!

THE MONSTERS OF THE MIDWAY—TEXAS VERSION
The Fort Worth Brewer **Bears** were named for a coach who had once played for the Chicago Bears.

CUTE LITTLE BABY BEARS

Five Texas schools call themselves **Cubs**, and four of the five (Brownfield, Clifton, Olney, and Roundtop-Carmine) are bear cubs. Roundtop-Carmine's girls' teams are the Cub-bettes. Alief Middle School, which feeds into Hastings High School (**Fighting Bears**), has a Cub mascot; Austin Middle School in Alamo (the Pharr-San Juan-Alamo **Bears**) has a **Bruin** mascot.

Pharr-San Juan-
Alamo
Bears

BIG WHITE BEARS

In Frost, you're in danger from **Polar Bears**, for goodness sake! Fortunately, Polar, in Kent County, is too small to have a high school or there'd probably be more of them loose.

Frost
Polar Bears

FAMOUS BEARS

Kimberly Tomes, Miss USA 1977, Houston Spring Branch
Dennis Rodman, basketball player, Dallas South Oak Cliff, 1976
Sheryl Swoopes, basketball player, Brownfield Cubs, 1989

Bowie Jackrabbits

Frisco Raccoons

More Native Critters

Some Texas animals are relatively innocuous—wouldn't hurt a fly. But you can find some pretty tough **Rabbits**—two kinds, the cute (maybe) bunnies (Atlanta) and the rangy rawboned **Jackrabbits** (Bowie, Forney, Graford, Ralls). There are **Raccoons** at Frisco (who resent being made into caps). The **Gophers** at Grand Prairie ("we will bury you") also seem harmless enough (operative word "seem"). Around San Saba, you may run into the Texas National Critter, the **Armadillo** . . . cute little fellers, but check those claws. Falls City, located near the junction of three watercourses, is a natural spot to find **Beavers.**

Other beasts have nastier reputations. **Badgers**, such as those at Ben Bolt-Palito Blanco, Lampasas, Merkel, and McCamey, are feisty critters. The South Texas brush country is the natural habitat of one of the state's least charming beasties, the **Javelinas** (Crystal City).

Falls City Battlin' Beavers

ASK ANY COONHOUND HOW TOUGH THEY ARE

For many years, the Frisco teams were the "Fighting Coons," but the school recently changed the name to "**Fighting Raccoons**" because the former name could have been taken to be derogatory to African-Americans. The name came from an event in 1924 when a boy asked the school to name its teams after his pet raccoon.

AND ON DEFENSE, THEY SIMPLY DUG IN

Grand Prairie **Gophers**—a coach was supposed to have said to the football team, "first and ten and go fer it again."

SO DID THEY

The San Saba **Armadillos** got their team nickname when a fan suggested that the football team was digging in like an armadillo. If you've ever tried to pull one by the tail out of its burrow, you'll understand what they're talking about. Even worse, the high school football field is allegedly laid out over a graveyard—so maybe you don't want to dig in too deep. We could ask actor Tommy Lee Jones. He came by that accent honestly, growing up in San Saba.

AND IF HIS NAME HAD BEEN HOBBS?

In the days before mascots, Atlanta had a coach named Ed Rabb. When it came time to choose a team name, they simply used his— the **Rabbits**.

THEY STAY IN THE COUNTRY SO THEY WON'T BE BADGERED BY PEOPLE

The ferocious Badgers may really be shy—none of the eight can be found in a town larger than 7,500, and only two of those little towns are even anywhere near a city of any size. Four of the eight are Class A schools.

Bruni Badgers

WILD PIGS

Javelinas (Crystal City) are collared peccaries, an aggressive type of wild hog that thrives in dry country. No one has picked their distant cousin, the Feral Pig, as a team name, even though that destructive beast is quietly taking over the state. Bucking a universal trend in Texas, one South Texas rancher quietly prays *against* rain. Javelinas thrive on dry weather; feral pigs die.

ASSOCIATED NAMES

Football stadiums are nearly always named either for some venerated person, usually a coach, or for the team. There are, for example, sixty or more football facilities in the state named "Eagle Stadium" or "Eagle Field." The same, in lesser numbers, can be said for Dragons and Tigers and Bulldogs and other mascots.

A few schools try variations on the theme—"The Bears Den" at Baird; "Excalibur Stadium," home of the El Paso Hanks Knights; "Wigwam Stadium" where the Seminole Indians host their guests; and Tolar's "The Rattler Pit."

"The Cotton Gin"—unofficial name for the gym at Robstown (Cottonpickers)

"The Herd"—the teams at Hereford (Whitefaces)

"The Cowboy Corral"—the football field at Happy (Cowboys)

"The Swarm from Stonewall County"—the Aspermont Hornets

"The Briar Patch"—gymnasium at Atlanta, where the teams are "Rabbits"

"The Dog House"—the workout facility at Abilene Wylie; teams are "Bulldogs"

"The Lariettes"—West Mesquite Wranglers drill team

"The Aristocats"—Bay City Black Cats drill team

"The Hornet's Nest"—the gymnasium at Athens

"The Bird's Nest"—the gymnasium for the St. Paul (Shiner) Cardinals

"Monoceras"—the drill team for New Braunfels Unicorns (names both mean "one horn")

"Bear Facts"—the Ursuline (Dallas) Bears school newspaper

"Colt Cavalry" and "Colt Kickers"—Arlington's boys spirit group and girls drill team

Kress Kangaroos

Exotics

Some beasties are exotics, not normally found in these parts—and we're not sure how some of them got loose here. For example, you don't usually run across **Gorillas** on the Texas Rolling Plains, but there's a lot of them around Trent. Hutto has a herd of **Hippos.** You might get kicked by a **Zebra** at Grandview or a **Kangaroo** at Killeen, Kress, or Weatherford. **Wolverines,** bad-tempered beasts whose range is usually restricted to more northern climes, can nevertheless be found at Houston Wilson, Springlake-Earth, Memorial (Alamo), and Penelope.

SINCE THEN, IT'S BEEN EVERY STUDENT'S DREAM TO BE A KANGAROO

Some say that Weatherford got to be **Kangaroos** after a boxing kangaroo escaped from a circus and punched out the superintendent, who then named the team that. Others say that they simply copied Austin College.

Weatherford Kangaroos

CAN YOU SAY "HUTTO HIPPOS" THREE TIMES REAL FAST? HOW ABOUT "HUTTO HIPPOPOTAMI"?

A hippopotamus escaped from a traveling circus near Austin and was found wallowing in a creek near Hutto. The creature was so belligerent and so hard to recapture that the folks at the school decided that would be a good symbol for their teams. The word is from the Greek, meaning "horse of the river."

Hutto Hippos

43

LADY GORILLAS ARE TOUGH ENOUGH FOR US.

The students at Trent High School picked the mascot **Gorillas** because they wanted something tough.

JUST DON'T CONFUSE THEM WITH THE REFEREES

Grandview **Zebras** got their name after a fire in 1920 when all athletic equipment burned.

Trent Gorillas

When their new team jerseys arrived, they turned out to be gold and white striped, so they took the name **Zebras** after the jerseys.

Grandview Zebras

Zephyr might consider changing their name from **Bulldogs** to Zebras. Not only would the alliteration work well, but there's a highly visible sign just outside town advertising a local exotic animal ranch. The sign features the picture of a zebra.

FAMOUS KANGAROOS

Mary Martin, actress, singer, Weatherford, 1931
Larry Hagman, actor, Weatherford, 1949

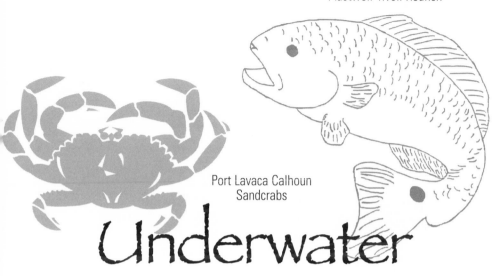

Austwell-Tivoli Redfish

Port Lavaca Calhoun
Sandcrabs

Underwater

You are not safe even when you are fishing Texas coastal waters. The Gulf swarms with predatory fish who would like to make you the next link in their food chain. THEY may be out HUMANING. **Redfish** (Austwell-Tivoli), **Tarpon** (Port Isabel), and **Marlin** (at Port Aransas and Houston's Madison high schools) are called "game fish"—but you can't be sure who's making the rules of THIS game.

"Jaws" was based on an event in New Jersey, but Texas coastal waters have their fair share of **Sharks** too, especially near Palacios and Sabine Pass. If you are swimming around Texas City, beware of **Stingarees**. Other denizens of the deep include **Stingrays** (League City Southshore Christian), **Sandcrabs** (Port Lavaca), and **Gators** (Dickinson). Salt water or fresh water, they'll get you either way.

BULLDOGGING SHARKS, ROPING JELLYFISH, RIDING WILD SEA HORSES

There used to be "tarpon rodeos" at Port Isabel, near the mouth of the Rio Grande. Now only a trickle of the Rio reaches the Gulf, so the **Tarpon** have gone elsewhere. But they are still present at Port Isabel High.

Port Isabel Tarpons

GO FIGURE

The only team of **Dolphins** in the state is in El Paso (El Paso School of Excellence), where there's really not a whole lot of salt water.

Marlin High School has the **Bulldog** for a mascot, not a Marlin. But then, Marlin is a couple of hundred miles from the Gulf. There's a team of **Gators** in Arlington, which doesn't seem to make much sense until you find out it's at Gateway School—the Gateway **Gators**.

HEADLINE:
SANDSHARKETTES WIN GAMES VS. RATTLERS

Palacios Sharks

The best derivative team name in the state belongs to the Palacios Junior High girls. Palacios High boys are Sharks; the girls are Sharkettes. Junior High boys are Sandsharks and the girls are SANDSHARKETTES! Oh yes, and the high school is at 100 Shark Drive; the junior high is at 200 Shark Drive.

FAMOUS GATORS
Tracy Scoggins, actress, Dickinson, 1970
Andre Ware, football player (Heisman Trophy, 1989), Dickinson, 1986

OFF COLORS

Some teams and towns have strange school colors:

Apple Springs	Blue and White
Bay City Black Cats	Blue and Gold
Blanco (Sp. for white)	Royal Blue and gold
Blue Ridge	Green and White
Carbon	Blue and White
Cotton Center	Black and Gold

El Dorado (the Golden One), **Alba-Golden,** and **Gold-Berg** do not have gold as one of their colors.

Greenville and **Greenwood** don't have green.

Redwater does not have red.

West Orange does not have orange.

Rosebud-Lott is Black and Gold.

Brownfield, Brownsboro, New Braunfels (German for brown stone) and **Brownwood** do not have brown, but **Brownsville Hanna** (the original high school) does.

Grapevine is red, white and blue; **Grapeland** is maroon, gray and white.

Blackwell is green and white.

W.T. White (Dallas), **White Oak, Whitehouse,** and **Whitesboro** all have white but **White Deer, Whiteface, Whitewright,** and **Whitesboro** do not.

Baytown Sterling has silver. (**Silverton** does not, nor does **Houston Sterling** nor does **Sterling City**)

The **Austin Maroons** have maroon. **Red Oak** has maroon (which is sort of red), **Goldthwaite** has gold, and **Colorado** (Spanish for red) **City** has red.

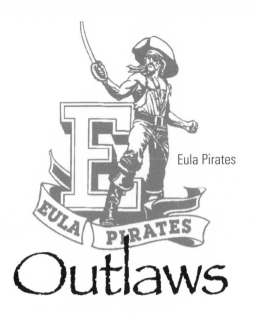

Eula Pirates

Outlaws

Of course, not all the dangers of Texas travel come from critters. There's some mighty ornery folks around, too. "Texas" might mean "friendly," but . . .

Jean LaFitte, the pirate, used to make Galveston Island his hideout, and it's likely other parts of the Texas coast have been infested by folks of his sort, too. And early Texas had its share of "filibusters," adventurers who came this way looking for wealth, power, and anything else they could take without working too hard at it. They were a pretty mean lot. There was a time when a strip of land along the

Brazoswood
Buccaneers

Louisiana border wasn't under the legal jurisdiction of any nation, and some tough hombres operated out of there. Even today, in the glass towers of Houston, Dallas, and Amarillo, there's a bunch called "corporate raiders" who have terrorized the country as far north as Wall Street—Ol' Boone Pickens and his allies. So we're not surprised to find out a few of these types still hang out in some of the smaller towns too. Maybe this is where we ought to include the Business and Management Magnet School of Dallas— they are the **Executives**.

Raiders have shown up all over the state. None of 'em are called the "Corporate Raiders" yet, but we got 'em in

Brownsville
Simón Rivera
Raiders

Red (Tyler Lee, Winnsboro), **Blue** (L.D. Bell of Hurst) and unmodified (twenty schools worth altogether—North Garland, Brownsville Rivera, Denton Ryan, Lumberton, and more). Variations of the name include **Buccaneers** (Brazoswood, Corpus Christi Miller), **Marauders** (Flower Mound Marcus), and **Pirates** (the ninth most frequently chosen mascot—including Center Point, Crawford, Lefors, Petrolia, Longview Pine Tree, Valentine, and Eula to name a few).

Lumberton
Raiders

WHY DOES A CHICKEN CROSS THE ROAD?
Race car driver-designer Carroll Shelby and chicken king Lonnie "Bo" Pilgrim were both Pittsburg **Pirates**.

FAMOUS RAIDERS
Michael Johnson, track, Dallas Skyline, 1986
Larry Johnson, basketball player (Mr. Basketball, 1987),
Dallas Skyline, 1987
Tommy Maddox, football player, Hurst Bell
Clyde Drexler, basketball player, Houston Sterling, 1980
Sandy Duncan, actress, Tyler Lee, 1964

FAMOUS PIRATES
Rick Perry, politician (Gov. of Texas), Paint Creek, 1969
Dat Nguyen, football player (Bednarik Award, 1998), Rockport

FAMOUS BUCCANEERS
Red McCombs, entrepreneur, philanthropist, Corpus Christi, 1945

Italy
Gladiators

Van Vandals

Ancient Warriors

We don't know just how these ancient warriors got out here to Texas in the 21st century, but so help me, there are places in the state occupied by **Vikings** (eleven schools including Austin Lanier, Irving Nimitz, Sugarland Dulles, Bryan), **Spartans** (Dallas Samuell, Austin St. Stephen's Episcopal, Houston Stratford), **Trojans** (the eighteenth most numerous name, with Beeville Jones, Tyler All Saints Episcopal, Cumby, and others), **Highlanders** (Fort Worth Eastern Hills, The Woodlands, El Paso Bel Air), the **Fighting Irish** (Shamrock), and **Vandals** (Van). And of course, the Highland Park **Scots.**

Dallas Highland Park
Scots

Bryan
Vikings

For sure, nobody will be able to get out of here without fighting somebody. We have a couple of teams of **Gladiators** (Italy and Roma, of course), for starters, and **Fighting Indians** (Jacksonville), **Fighting Owls** (Joshua), **Fighting Texans** (Corpus Christi Ray), **War Eagles** (Conroe Oak Ridge), **Fighting Eagles** (DeSoto, among others), **Fighting Hornets** (Gatesville), **Warriors** (the eleventh most popular mascot), **Battlin' Billies** (Fredericksburg), **Fighting Rams** (Houston Kashmere), **Fighting Cowboys** (Brownsville Porter) . . . and those are the nice ones.

BEWARE OF GREEKS BEARING GIFTS

Why are there so many Trojans? There used to be an old saying that a really industrious person "worked like a Trojan." But Texas has no particular connection with an ancient kingdom in western Asia Minor whose main claim to fame was that they lost a war. Only the town of Troy has a clear relationship to the name, but alliteration may explain why Trinidad, Trinity, Trinity Christian of Addison, and Trinity Valley of Fort Worth are all **Trojans**.

THE SCANDINAVIAN CONNECTION

Are all those Vikings schools named by admirers of the Minnesota pro football team? Probably not, but until 2005, the Minnesota Vikings WERE owned by Red McCombs . . . who lives in San Antonio. And shouldn't Woden be the Vikings? That's the Norse-Teutonic god who gave his name to Wodensday.

North Dallas teams were originally named the Vikings. Somebody, it is said, thought Vikings kept bulldogs as suitably vicious pets. As our informant at the school put it, "Bulldogs stuck, Vikings drowned."

SCOT HOTSHOTS

The Highland Park **Scots** football team had a pretty good backfield in 1942 and 1943, with Bobby Layne at quarterback and Ewell D. Walker, Jr., at halfback. Doak Walker won the Heisman and both are now in the NFL Hall of Fame. The annual award for the nation's best college running back is the Doak Walker Award.

¡HOLA, AMIGO! HOOT, MON!

El Paso Bel Air got the name **Highlanders** when the school superintendent visited Scotland one year and was enchanted by the country. Since Bel Air sits in the hills overlooking the Rio Grande Valley, it's not entirely inappropriate. They have Scottish festivals, a bagpipe band, and study groups organized as "clans," such as the Glasgow Clan, the Inverness Clan, the Edinburgh Clan, and so on. The bagpipe band created a small controversy a few years back when

El Paso
Bel Air
Highlanders

51

the male students refused to wear the obligatory kilts. But someone dared to be the first and now the whole band, some of the male staff, and even a few community members wear them. It's strange to find this nest of Scotsmen on the Mexican border.

Almost as out of place are the El Paso Cathedral teams who are called the **Irish**.

FAMOUS SCOTS
Bill Clements, businessman, politician (Gov. of Texas)
Highland Park, 1934
Vera Jayne Peers (Jayne Mansfield), actress,* Highland Park, 1950
Angie Harmon, actress,* Highland Park, 1990

FAMOUS TROJANS
Aaron Spelling, producer, Dallas Forest Avenue, 1939

FAMOUS SPARTANS
Craig James, football player, broadcaster, Houston Stratford

FAMOUS VIKINGS
Jeremy Wariner, 2004 Olympic 400 meter gold medalist,
Arlington Lamar

*This is the **Scots**-*Law and Order* connection. Harmon starred on the original TV series for several years while Mansfield's daughter, Mariska Hargitay, plays the female lead on *Law and Order: SVU*.

Harker Heights
Knights

Boys Ranch
Roughriders

Soldiers

The military tradition is strong in the state. With seven percent of the country's population, Texans account for nine percent of the U.S. military. The highest ranks are the **Generals** (Houston Lee, Houston MacArthur, Richardson Alexander). South Garland has the **Colonels**. The closest thing we have to the meanest of them all, the sergeants, is Edinburg's **Sergeanette** pep squad.

But Texas is ready for war. We have **Troopers** (El Paso Eastwood—near Fort Bliss), **Patriots** (Dallas Jefferson, Veteran's Memorial of Mission), **Volunteers** (Arlington Bowie, San Antonio Lee), **Minutemen** (Memorial of San Antonio), **Leathernecks** (Harlingen's Marine Military Academy), and **Soldiers** (Believers Academy of San Antonio). Representing an old-fashioned way of war, there are **Swordsmen** (Garland Christian Academy) and **Knights** (most of which are church schools—Bellaire Episcopal, Lakewood Presbyterian, Wichita Falls Notre Dame, Seagoville First Assembly Christian, but also Dallas Kimball). The most revered of the knights are the **Paladins** (Providence Classical School of Spring). The knights can ride to battle on **Warhorses** (Devine) or **Chargers** (El Paso Jesus Chapel, Dallas Shelton,

The Woodlands
College Park
Cavaliers

San Antonio Churchill
Chargers

El Paso Eastwood Troopers

53

Midland Trinity), which are horses, not people with too many credit cards. A new recruit to this army is the **Cavalier** of The Woodlands College Park High School.

Center
Roughriders

Waco Connally's teams are called **Cadets.** The school's name comes from a nearby pilot training center called Connally Field. San Antonio's Theodore Roosevelt High School honors the Spanish-American War cavalry unit that Teddy recruited in San Antonio—the **Rough Riders.** There are others of the same name at Center and Boys Ranch. They have **Conquerors** at Fort Worth Calvary Academy and **Conquistadores** at El Paso Del Valle.

THAT'S THE SECOND THING YOU LEARN IN THE ARMY—NEVER VOLUNTEER FOR ANYTHING.

Bowie chose **Volunteers** for its mascot after a teacher quoted a famous saying to the effect that the greatness of a city was to be found in its volunteers. Maybe Gonzales should be the Volunteers too, in honor of the 32 men from their town who marched to certain death in the Alamo in 1836. (Oh, and what's the FIRST thing you learn in the army? Never call a sergeant "sir.")

Arlington
James Bowie
Volunteers

Houston MacArthur
Generals

HE WAS HALF-WAY THERE ALREADY

U.S. Attorney-General Alberto Gonzales graduated from Houston MacArthur High School in 1973. MacArthur's mascot is the **General**, so Gonzales was already an attorney General from the time he got his law degree.

DEVINE EQUINES

Devine's **Warhorses** derive their name from the 1923-1924 football season. Their coach that year was Robert C. ("Warhorse") Tate. By the end of the season, they were called "Warhorse's boys," and the name was officially adopted at the banquet celebrating the end of the football season.

FAMOUS KNIGHTS

Mia Hamm, soccer, Wichita Falls Notre Dame
Tom Kite, golf, Austin McCallum, 1968
Jay Arnette, basketball player (USOC Hall of Fame),
Austin McCallum

MIXED AT BIRTH?

Jersey Village of Houston is not the Jerseys; **Falfurrias** is.

Whiteface is not the Herefords but **Hereford** is the Whitefaces.

Cotton Center is not the Cottonpickers. That's **Robstown**.

Plains is not the Plainsmen, but **Lubbock Monterey** is.

Redwater is not the Sharks; that's **Palacios** or **Sabine Pass**.

The Bells women's teams are the Lady Panthers, not the Belles. The Belles are **Falfurrias's** women's teams.

West is not the Westerners; **Lubbock High** is.

St. Gerard (San Antonio) and **Westside Monastery** (Houston) are Royals, but **Grandfalls-Royalty** has Cowboys and **Royal** (Brookshire) has Falcons.

Shamrock is not the Shamrocks—that's **Incarnate Word** (San Antonio).

The name Ambassadors belongs to **Bethesda School** of Fort Worth, not to **Ambassadors of Christ School**, also in Fort Worth.

Dublin is not the Celtics; that name belongs to **Holy Trinity Catholic** of Temple. On the other hand, **Shamrock** IS the Fighting Irish.

Marfa Shorthorns

San Antonio MacArthur Brahmas

Ranch Life

The Lone Star State is famous for its ranches . . . but they're not all like the Southfork—no sirree! Some of 'em are plumb dangerous. Among the livestock that you'd better look out for are herds of nasty-tempered cattle—**Longhorns**, mostly, (Amarillo Caprock, Harper, George West, Lazbuddie, Dallas White) but with a mixture of other breeds too—**Shorthorns** (Schulenberg, Marfa), **Whitefaces** (Hereford), **Brahmas** (pronounced "Brimmers" around here), or just plain **Steers** (who have good reason to be mad.) You'll encounter **Brahmas** at Stockdale, East Bernard, and Houston Furr, among other places. **Steers** are found in West Texas at places like Farwell, Big Spring, and Graham. You'll even see an occasional **Maverick**, which is bovine, not human, at San Antonio Madison, Eastland, and Pearsall. The **Bulls** (Bridgeport) and **Toros** (Laredo Cigarroa) assure that the breed will remain aggressive.

Bridgeport Bulls

There are some pretty ornery fellers looking out after them, too. You have to watch out for **Cowboys** (Happy, Premont, Edna, Dallas Carter), **Buckaroos** (Breckenridge), **Vaqueros** (San Diego, Sierra Blanca), and **Punchers** (Mason). They'll be riding (or *trying* to ride) **Broncos** (Clarendon, Denton, Sonora), **Colts** (Arlington, Houston Worthing), **Stallions** (North Mesquite), and **Mustangs** (the sixth most popular name, including Denver City,

West Mesquite Wranglers

Nixon-Smiley Mustangs

57

Sweetwater Mustangs

Sweetwater, Andrews, Fort Hancock, Corpus Christi King, San Antonio Jefferson, Houston Christian). If it was a dude ranch, you might find **Pacers**, too, like at Waco Parkview Christian Academy.

AIN'T NEVER BEEN A HOSS THAT COULDN'T BE RODE; AIN'T NEVER BEEN A COWBOY THAT COULDN'T BE THROWED

You'd think Wichita Falls Rider might change that, but they're the **Raiders**, not the Riders. If the horse has a burr under its saddle, it might still be bucking. And wouldn't you know—there is a team of **Burrs** at Chinquapin School near Houston.

WE'VE GOT A BEEF WITH PORT LAVACA AND GANADO

Hereford Whitefaces

There ought to be some kind of cattle name for Port Lavaca (Spanish for "the cow"), Ganado (Spanish for "cattle"), or Jersey Village. Hereford has a cattle name. They are **Whitefaces**, which refers to the markings of the Hereford breed.

MAYBE THEY HAD IT RIGHT THE FIRST TIME

Bridgeport **Bulls** were originally "Bullies" until they shortened it in 1968. The girls' teams were "Sissies" until recently, when they became "Lady Bulls?"

MAVERICKS

Marshall Mavericks

A San Antonio cattleman named Sam Maverick sometimes neglected to brand his calves. Thus when they had a roundup, Maverick could claim that any unbranded yearling was his. People around San Antonio sarcastically referred to an unbranded cow as "one of Maverick's." The verb "mavericking" meant something just this side of rustling. The name evolved to mean anyone who was excessively independent, such as in "Top Gun" or the James Garner TV series.

58

HOOK 'EM

Harper Longhorns

The longhorns are descendants of escaped Spanish cattle which multiplied in the brush country of South Texas. After the Civil War, impoverished Southerners could, at considerable risk to life and limb, round them up and drive them north to the railheads in Missouri and Kansas. No capital was needed except enough for a "ten-dollar horse and a forty-dollar saddle," and perhaps a sack of beans. While the longhorns didn't have much beef on them, they were hardy enough (and mean enough) to survive the long trail drives. When railroads came to Texas, there was no longer a need for these brush-wise critters, and they were replaced by, among others, the Herefords, who could pack a lot of meat on their frames, even if they might not have been good travelers.

Longhorns are popular in the state, with over two dozen manifestations, making it the fourteenth most used mascot. (See Appendix A.)

A MIXED MARRIAGE

Once upon a time, a long, long time ago, the town of Agua Dulce was trying to settle on a high school mascot. One group of parents wanted to honor the University of Texas while another group wanted to celebrate Texas A&M. The result of this debate can be seen today—the Agua Dulce **Longhorns** wear Maroon and White (Aggie colors). At least, that's one explanation.

Agua Dulce Longhorns

THEY COULD HAVE BEEN NAMED FOR A PLAYER NAMED "CRACKER."

The Graham **Steers** were named, it is said, for a player nicknamed "Steer."

MUSTANG WINE

The Grapevine **Mustangs** are the namesake of mustang grapes, a wild variety that grows in several parts of Texas, including the Metroplex area.

MOTHERS, DON'T LET YOUR DAUGHTERS GROW UP TO BE COWGIRLS

No school that has adopted **Cowboys** for its male teams has used Lady Cowboys for the female version. They are always **Cowgirls**. In fact, there may be more Cowgirls than Cowboys, since Mason has **Punchers** for the boys and **Cowgirls** as the female counterpart.

Mason Punchers

FAMOUS MUSTANGS

Robert F. Curl, Jr., chemist (1996 Nobel Prize), San Antonio Jefferson, 1950
Kyle Rote, football player, San Antonio Jefferson
Jim Lehrer, journalist, San Antonio Jefferson
Tommy Nobis, football player, San Antonio Jefferson
Sammy Baugh, football player, Sweetwater, 1933
Clyde ("Bulldog") Turner, football player, Sweetwater
B.J. Thomas, singer, Rosenberg Lamar
Michael Dell, entrepreneur, Houston Spring Branch Memorial
Max Lucado, minister, writer, Andrews
Chad Campbell, golfer, Andrews

FAMOUS MAVERICKS

Bill Moyers, journalist, Marshall, 1952
Y.A. Tittle, football player, Marshall
Lady Bird Johnson, first lady, conservationist, Marshall
George Strait, singer, Pearsall

FAMOUS COWBOYS

Steve Williams (Stone Cold Steve Austin), wrestler, Edna, 1982

FAMOUS BRONCOS

Shirley Cothran, Miss America 1975, Denton, 1973

Alamo Heights
Mules

Poteet Aggies

Farm Life

Life on the farm is kinda laid back, right? Not hardly, city boy! The Roscoe **Plowboys** could be fixin' to plow you under. There are two teams of **Mules** available to pull those plows (San Antonio Alamo Heights and Muleshoe). Of course, they may be too stubborn to cooperate very much. When it comes time to gather the crops, the Pampa **Harvesters** could be at your service, or . . . they may want to cut you off at the knees. Texas has regular **Farmers** (well, not too regular) at Farmersville (of course) and Lewisville as well as the **Aggies** at Poteet.

Lewisville Farmers

Falfurrias Fightin'
Jerseys

And then there are the dreaded Robstown **Cotton-pickers**.

The Falfurrias **Jerseys** bear the name of the dairy cattle that were imported to South Texas around 1910. Falfurrias became a major dairy center with a famous creamery.

THE INSPIRATION FOR THE BEVERLY HILLBILLIES?

Kathryn Grandstaff (later actress Kathy Grant—Mrs. Bing Crosby) was once the ace of the Cottonpicker tennis team as a freshman. In fact, the school says that she remains the only four-year letter winner Robstown has ever had.

YOU CAN TAKE THE BOY OUT OF THE COUNTRY, BUT YOU CAN'T TAKE THE COUNTRY OUT OF THE BOY.... OR GIRL EITHER

Roscoe **Plowboys** may have been named after the John Tarleton Agricultural College teams, who were allegedly Plowboys, when a number of Roscoe alums attended the Stephenville school. Then the school (now Tarleton State University) changed its mascot to Texans, but Roscoe kept the name. And the girls' teams are not the Lady Plowboys (thank goodness) but the **Plowgirls** while the Tarleton women's teams are now the TexAnns.

Roscoe Plowboys

MULISHNESS

It's easy to see how Muleshoe got its **Mule** mascot, but the Alamo Heights **Mules** in the middle of San Antonio is a bit more obscure. The name, it seems, came from the football coach, Earl "Mule" Frazier. As a schoolboy hurdler, Frazier set several state records running barefooted. Recruited to Texas A&M, he refused to wear running shoes and had to transfer to a more accommodating coach at Baylor. The Aggie coach swore Frazier was "as stubborn as a mule" over the incident. The Alamo Heights football team won district in 1926 under Frazier's leadership, and were known as "Mule's boys."

The name stuck. Boy, did it ever—the gym is "the Muledome," the baseball field is "the Mule Yard," the softball field is "the Lady Mules' Field," the newspaper is "The Hoofprint," and the booster clubs are "the Mule Team" and "the Mulepushers."

FAMOUS HARVESTERS
Randy Matson, shot put record holder, Pampa
Zac Thomas, football player, Pampa

FAMOUS FARMERS
Walt Garrison, football player, Lewisville
Charles ("Tex") Watson, Manson gang, Farmersville, 1964
Audie Murphy, war hero, actor, Farmersville

FAMOUS COTTONPICKERS
Gene Upshaw, football player, union leader, Robstown, 1963
Marvin Upshaw, football player, businessman, Robstown, 1964
Solomon Ortiz, politician (U.S. House of Representatives),
Robstown, 1951

FAMOUS MULES
Ponce Cruse (Heloise), columnist,
San Antonio Alamo Heights, 1969

HEADLINES

How might a newspaper headline read when these two teams meet? Match them up. For example, (1) is H—"At home on the range," where the Deer and the Antelopes play.

__H__ (1) Whiteface (Antelopes) at White Deer (Bucks)

_____ (2) Kerrville (Antlers) and New Braunfels (Unicorns)

_____ (3) Roscoe (Plowboys) and Lewisville (Farmers)

_____ (4) Seguin (Matadors) and Bridgeport (Bulls)

_____ (5) Texline (Tornadoes) and Memphis (Cyclones)

_____ (6) Diboll (Lumberjacks) and White Oak (Roughnecks)

_____ (7) Dallas Carter (Cowboys) against Denton (Broncos)

_____ (8) Snook (Bluejays) and Bridge City (Cardinals)

_____ (9) Wichita Falls Hirschi (Huskies) vs. Abilene Wylie (Bulldogs)

_____ (10) Dallas Kimball (Knights) vs. El Paso Hanks (Knights)

A. To determine who's top dog
B. It's a rodeo
C. To go round and round
D. To beat plowshares into swords.
E. Gather in the lists for a joust
F. To lock horns
G. Will establish pecking order.
H. At home on the range tonight
I. In barroom brawl
J. Plan corrida

San Angelo
Lake View
Chiefs

Donna Redskins

Indians

In picking the fiercest mascot they could think of, a lot of schools paid tribute to the Native American tribes who disputed the spread of the frontier across Texas. Many Texas town names reflect that heritage and their high schools carry the name **Indians** (the ninth most common name). Cherokee, Comanche, Lipan, and Seminole are Texas towns named for tribes. Pawnee, in South Texas, also has Indians but they now only go through eighth grade so the young Pawnee Indians then go to neighboring high schools to become **Trojans**, **Bulldogs**, **Badgers**, **Lions**, and **Bobcats**. Jim Ned (in Tuscola), Nocona, and Quanah were famous chiefs. The town of Paint Rock is named for inscribed stones near the community. All these schools, and more, have **Indians** as their team totem. Naturally, Cleveland is also the **Indians**.

Lipan Indians

Some teams bear tribal names—**Apaches** (Gonzales, Antonian Prep of San Antonio), **Comanches** (Shiner, West Texas of Stinnett), **Kiowas** (Booker), and **Yeguas** (Somerville). San Antonio Sam Houston was once the **Cherokees**. But no high school has picked the tribe for which the state was named—Tejas. Maybe no one knew how to pronounce it, and besides, who wants a team that is "friendly"? On the other hand, no team is named the Karankawas. That coastal tribe was maybe a little too fierce—they were reputed to be cannibals. The Indian motif is also found in **Chiefs** (Crosbyton, San Angelo Lake View), **Chieftains** (Friona), **Braves** (Nevada Community, Iraan), and **Redskins** (Houston Lamar, Donna).

Arlington Martin Warriors

The name **Warriors** (the twelfth most used mascot) sometimes applies to Indians and sometimes not. About half of the occurrences of this name are from private schools, and their logos are normally Roman or Greek. Most of the public schools which use Warrior refer to Native Americans. Sometimes the name is soft-pedaled;

Warren Warriors

Plano Williams (**Warriors**) has nothing Indian on its website, but its drill team is called the Chey-Annes.

THE REAL INDIANS ARE WILDCATS

The only school with a substantial number of real Native Americans (Big Sandy of Dallardsville, serving the Alabama-Coushatta reservation) calls its teams **Wildcats.** Nowadays, less than a fourth of students are Native Americans, but fifty years ago, their state championship basketball teams were almost totally Native American.

INSPIRATION

Four schools in Collin County went together in the fall of 1948 to create the new Community High School at Nevada. The administration allowed the first graduating class to pick the school song, the colors, and the mascot. The students picked **Braves** because they were "courageous, fearless, bold, and undaunted," just like the teams would be.

FLOW GENTLY, SWEET YEGUA

Somerville's teams are named either for the Yegua tribe which once inhabited the area or for the neighboring creek that named after the tribe. So, their theme could either be Native American or watery. (On second thought, not all Texas "creeks" have water very often.)

FAMOUS CHEROKEES

Kenneth Starr, lawyer, prosecutor, San Antonio Sam Houston, 1962

FAMOUS REDSKINS
Linda Smith Ellerbee, journalist, Houston Lamar, 1962
Tommy Tune, dancer, director, Houston Lamar, 1957

FAMOUS WARRIORS
Kandace Krueger, Miss USA 2001, Round Rock Westwood

FAMOUS CHIEFS
Henry, Jojo, and Ringo Garza (Los Lonely Boys), musicians,
San Angelo Lake View

MORE HEADLINES

Match them up.

_____(1) Poolville (Monarchs) and San Antonio St Gerard (Royals)
_____(2) Fort Worth Boswell (Pioneers) and Waxahachie (Indians).
_____(3) El Paso Loreto (Angels) and Presidio (Blue Devils)
_____(4) Cy-Fair (Lady Bobcats) and Houston Sam Houston (Lady Tigers)
_____(5) Sugarland Dulles (Vikings) and Honey Grove (Warriors)
_____(6) Italy (Gladiators) and Trinidad (Trojans)
_____(7) South Garland (Colonels) vs. Richardson Alexander (Generals)
_____(8) Richland Springs (Coyotes) vs. Austin Waldorf (Roadrunners)
_____(9) Knippa (Rockcrushers) vs. Rockwall (Yellowjackets)
_____(10) Sabine Pass (Sharks) vs. Port Lavaca (Sandcrabs)

A. The Battle of Armageddon set for tonight.
B. The classic cartoon chase—who will win?
C. Circle the wagons—tonight it's _____
D. Jaws and Claws
E. Who's the sweetest fighter? _____ will decide tonight
F. It's a catfight . . .
G. To determine king of the hill
H. to cross swords.
I. The Old Army Game
J. The irresistible force meets the immovable object:

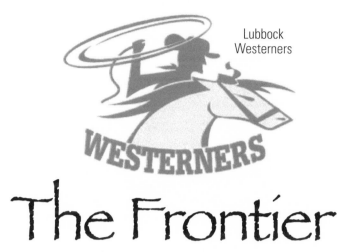
Lubbock
Westerners

The Frontier

Several Texas school nicknames commemorate the pioneers who moved across the frontier in the 19th century. On the high plains in Lubbock, there are **Westerners** (Lubbock High) and **Plainsmen** (Lubbock Monterey). You had to be tough to survive on the Llano Estacado, and these teams sure enough fill the bill. Among the **Pioneers** are Fort Worth Boswell and Granbury's Happy Hill Academy. Then we have the **Trailblazers** at El Paso Americas and Cedar Park's Twin Lakes Fellowship School.

Lubbock Monterey
Plainsmen

Most folks may think they're nearly extinct, but here and there you're gonna come across herds of **Buffaloes** (Cross Plains, Forsan, Giddings, Houston Milby, Stanton) and **Bison** (Dallas Sunset, and, naturally, Buffalo). West Texas was the southern end of the Great Plains buffalo range and buffalo hunters were among the first Europeans to try to survive there. (Near Snyder, a buffalo hunter named J. Wright Mooar killed a rare and revered white buffalo, and a statue of the beast stands in the courthouse square . . . but Snyder's teams are, for some reason, **Tigers**.) If you've never been in front of a herd, take our advice—you'd better look out; those critters will stampede right over you.

San Antonio
Fox Tech
Buffaloes

69

O GIVE ME A HOME WHERE THE BUFFALO ROAM

The football stadium in Florence, home of the **Buffaloes**, is called "Stampede Field." (See, we TOLD you there might be a stampede.)

FLOAT LIKE A BUFFALO, STING LIKE A BEE

Haltom's team name was picked from a long list of nominations by the class of 1932. The two finalists were Buffaloes and Bees. The class chose to be called **Buffaloes**.

FAMOUS WESTERNERS

Buddy Holly, singer, Lubbock HS, 1955
Mac Davis, singer, Lubbock HS, 1960
Natalie Maines, singer (Dixie Chicks), Lubbock HS, 1992

FAMOUS PLAINSMEN

Barry Corbin, actor, Lubbock Monterey, 1958

B.F. Terry
Rangers

Laredo
Cigarroa
Toros

Five Flags Over Texas

(Not to add to the France-bashing, but the French didn't really make that big of an impact in Texas during La Salle's brief time in the area.)

Spanish

The Spanish heritage in Texas is recollected in numerous town and school names, but also in mascots. El Paso Del Valle has **Conquistadores** as its team name, remembering the Spaniards who explored the state. Lubbock's Estacado High School is named for the Staked (estacado) Plains traversed first by the Francisco Coronado expedition in 1540. Lubbock also celebrates Coronado's name with a high school. Amarillo Palo Duro is the **Dons**, honoring the early Spanish landowners.

Amarillo Palo Duro
Dons

Mexican

Texas began its political life as a province of New Spain and gained a measure of independence when all of Mexico, including the northeastern state called "Coahuila y Tejas," successfully revolted against Spanish rule in the 1820s. Through its own later revolution against Mexico in 1836, Texas became a de facto sovereign republic, though its southwestern boundaries were more than a little indefinite. But

Sierra Blanca Vaqueros

the Hispanic tradition in Texas remained strong, as reflected by the names of towns and streams. It shows up also in team names—**Toros** (Laredo Cigarroa), **Matadors** (including Seguin, Lubbock Estacado, Motley County), **Coyotes** (Anna, La Joya, Wichita Falls), **Javelinas** (Crystal City), **Lobos** (Cisco, Houston Chavez, Monahans, others), and **Vaqueros** (San Diego, Sierra Blanca).

Texas

A number of schools in recent years have adopted the name "**Texans**," among them Pasadena's Sam Rayburn High, Wimberley, and Houston of Arlington. Though we can't imagine that the unadorned name is too tame, Corpus Christi Ray made its team the "**Fighting Texans**." Numerous schools bear the names of heroes of the Texas revolution—Sam Houston (in Arlington, Houston, San Antonio), Stephen F. Austin (in El Paso, Austin, Houston, Port Arthur, Sugarland), Juan Seguín (in Arlington and Seguin), and four men who died in the Alamo: James Bowie (in Austin, El Paso, Arlington, Simms), James B. Bonham (Bonham), William B. Travis (Austin), and David Crockett (Crockett, Austin).

Arlington
Sam Houston
Texans

Sugarland Clements
Rangers

The famous Texas **Rangers** (Perryton, Baytown Sterling, Austin's Texas School for the Deaf) are honored at a number of schools. The organization began for frontier defense during the Republic period, served as a military unit during the 1846 war with Mexico, and still exists as a law enforcement body. (One riot, one Ranger.) However, they are not universally admired among Hispanics in South Texas and no school in the southwest quadrant of the state bears the name.

Confederate

The Confederacy is not forgotten in Texas, either. No less than a dozen Texas schools named their teams **Rebels**, but not one Texas high school team is called Yankees. Surprised? President Jeff Davis is remembered by a Houston school that bears his name. Houston and Austin have schools named Reagan. Then there's Reagan County High School in Big Lake. But they're not named for Ronnie—they commemorate John H. Reagan, a Texan in the Confederate cabinet.

Buda Hays Rebels

The greatest of all the southern heroes was Robert E. Lee, who served in Texas until just before the Civil War began. The Houston Lee **Generals**, the Midland Lee **Rebels**, and the San Antonio Lee **Volunteers** clearly represent the Paladin of the Confederacy. Less obviously, Tyler Lee has **Red Raiders**, the town of Robert Lee has **Steers,** and Baytown Lee has **Ganders**, but that's another story.

B.F. Terry High School of Rosenberg bears the name **Rangers**, which applies here rather than in the state category. B.F. Terry organized a cavalry regiment for the Civil War, a group known as Terry's Texas Rangers.

United States

Lakeview
Centennial
Patriots

Texans may not be Yankees, but they *are* good Americans. Several schools have **Patriots** (Dallas Jefferson and Veterans Memorial of Mission, appropriately enough, plus Valley High School of Turkey, and Lakeview-Centennial of Garland) and one has **Minutemen** (Memorial of San Antonio). The closest we can come to Yankees is the pep squad from Lakeview Centennial—the Yankee Doodle Sweethearts.

VIVA EL PRESIDENTE

Lots of Texas schools are named for presidents, one way or another. The obvious examples are Eisenhower of Aldine, Ronald Reagan of San Antonio, LBJ of Austin and LBJ in Johnson City, George Bush of Houston (for the elder Bush), James Madison of Dallas, Thomas Jefferson of San Antonio, Lincoln of Dallas, Theodore Roosevelt of San Antonio, Franklin D. Roosevelt of Dallas, William Howard Taft of San Antonio, and John Tyler of Tyler.

But there are more. Jeff Davis of Houston is named for the president of the Confederacy and the Sam Houston schools are named for a man who was twice president of Texas. Anson in Jones County is named for Anson Jones, the last president of the Republic of Texas, and Mirabeau B. Lamar High School in Houston bears the name of still another Texas president. La Joya has two 9th-10th grade schools named for three presidents—Jimmy Carter, and Benito Juárez-Abraham Lincoln. Santa Anna doesn't make this list—the town's namesake was an Indian chief, not the much-vilified Mexican president. Not one of those schools calls its teams Presidents.

NASALLY INCORRECT

No school honors the president who really brought Texas into the Union—James Knox Polk. Don't you think the Polk Polekats would have a nice ring to it?

A NATURAL RIVALRY

The towns of Nixon (**Mustangs**) and Kenedy (**Lions**), only thirty miles apart in South Texas, are *not* named for the 1960 presidential opponents.

GUVS

A few Texas governors also have schools named for them. Sam Houston was a governor, in addition to having been president. Gov. Ross Sterling has two schools named for him, one in Houston and one in Baytown. Gov. John Connally is remembered by a school bearing his name in Austin. Sugarland's Clements High School honors Gov. Bill

74

Clements. However, no Texas school name celebrates one of the greatest of them all, Gov. Jim Hogg. All he got was a county. (And yes, he *did* have a daughter named Ima, and no, she did *not* have sisters named Ura or Vera.) What mascot comes to mind for a future Jim Hogg High School?

WHERE ARE THE LEGAL EAGLES?

Five Supreme Court justices are honored in Texas high school names. They are John Marshall (one school in Marshall and another in San Antonio), Thurgood Marshall (Missouri City), Earl Warren (San Antonio), and Sandra Day O'Connor (Helotes). Since William Howard Taft (San Antonio) was chief justice as well as president, he belongs on this list too. But none of the schools have judicial names—they are **Mavericks**, **Rams**, **Bulldogs**, **Warriors**, **Panthers**, and **Raiders** respectively. The town of Taft, near Corpus Christi, is named for the president/chief-justice's brother, so it doesn't count on this list. We suppose names like Lawyers or Judges don't carry the right connotation.

So, where are the "legal eagles?" Well, you can find them in Dallas, where the magnet School of Government and Law has adopted the **Eagle** as its mascot!

T FOR TEXAS, T FOR TENNESSEE

There are even some Texas schools named after a governor of Tennessee!!! . . . Well, OK, it's Sam Houston, but he *was* governor of Tennessee briefly before he came to Texas.

FAMOUS FIGHTING TEXANS
Farrah Fawcett, actress, Corpus Christi Ray, 1965

FAMOUS REBELS
Laura Bush, First Lady of the U.S., Midland Lee, 1965

West Hardin Oilers

Munday Moguls

Royalty and Working Folk

Texas has always been noted for its egalitarian ways, but we do have some royalty among us. The **Barons** may be found at St. Mary's Hall of San Antonio. The more generic term **Royals** describes St. Gerard's of San Antonio and Houston Westside Monastery.

Moguls are not the snow bumps so beloved by skiers, but the warriors (the name derived from "Mongols") who swept through the passes of northern India, overthrowing the native princes and establishing their reign there for centuries. One of the Moguls built the Taj Mahal. The name also came to apply to Englishmen who made their fortunes administering British rule of India. There is a very successful bunch of **Moguls** at Munday.

One school calls its teams **Yoemen**, evoking the basic English medieval middle class (yeomen) who won the wars against France with their longbows. That's Yoe High School in Cameron. Other teams bear the names of every-day occupations, and that's not counting the afore-mentioned **Cowboys** and **Farmers**. Brazosport has **Exporters**, a play on the town name rather than a hint that they ship lots of stuff out of the country.

Brazosport Exporters

West Hardin's and Pearland's teams are the **Oilers**, and West Columbia, Sundown and White Oak all are **Roughnecks**, referring to the guys who do the dirty work in the oil patch. (Can we count "Wildcat(ter)s" in this group? Maybe so. One source said that that was indeed the origin of the nickname for the Humble **Wildcats**. Humble was an oil boom town.)

Knippa Fighting Rockcrushers

You're not likely to find a team of **Lumberjacks** on the high plains, but Diboll, in the Piney Woods of East Texas, has them. Knippa, on the southern edge of the Hill Country, boasts teams of **Purple Rockcrushers**. You can't get any tougher than that. The name of the

Diboll Lumberjacks

Voks of San Antonio Lanier harkens back to the time when Lanier was a vocational school. Their gear-wheel logo evokes the spirit of industry. (See page 122.) Santa Anna's **Mountaineers** are so named because the town sits at the foot of a prominent hill.

TEXAS NOBILITY

We don't count Cattle Barons or Stock-and-Bond Kings as real royalty. On the other hand, maybe John ("the Duke") Wayne WAS real royalty. At least he was treated that way when he came to Brackettville to film "The Alamo."

Texas does boast some near-royalty—Joe "King" Carrasco, the Tex-Mex rock and roll singer; "King" Charlie Hillard, the Fort Worth car dealer; and Nolan Ryan, whose last name is Irish for "Little King." In Texas, he's not "little." Speaking of Ryans, Rice University once had a regal quarterback tandem of Frank Ryan and King Hill. Both of them had long post-college careers in the NFL.

Then there's our Rajah. Rogers ("The Rajah") Hornsby, the baseball immortal, grew up in Winters, Texas. Twenty years younger and he would have been a **Blizzard**.

CROWNED HEADS

Some of our ladies have worn crowns. Actress Sissy Spacek was Homecoming Queen at Quitman. She played the antithesis of that role in "Carrie." Senator Kay Bailey Hutchinson was Homecoming Queen at LaMarque.

Jo-Carroll Dennison of Tyler John Tyler (1942), Shirley Cothran of Denton (1975), and Phyllis George of Denison (1971) all were crowned "Miss America."

And "Miss USA?" A whole run of them starting with Kimberly Tomes (1977 of Houston Spring Branch High School), followed by Laura Martinez Herring (1985, born in Mexico, schooled in San Antonio, graduated high school in Switzerland), Christy Fichtner (1986 from Dallas), Michelle Royer (1987 from Keller), Courtney Gibbs (1988 from Fort Worth), Gretchen Polhemus (1989 from Fort Worth), and Kandace Krueger (2001, a graduate of Round Rock's Westwood HS). The Texan who won Miss USA in 1995 had to yield up her crown—because she went on to be Miss Universe—Chelsi Smith, a 1991 graduate of Deer Park High. Yes, she was a real **Deer**. Fichtner was first runner-up for Miss Universe in her year and Royer was second runner-up in 1987.

REGAL SCHOOLS

We have some schools with royal names, but they don't have "royal" teams—Grandfalls-Royalty **Cowboys**, and Royal (Brookshire) **Falcons**, and the Manor (as in "the Lord of the . . . ") **Mustangs**. Other nobility could have come from Kingsville (but they are **Brahmas**), Queen City (**Bulldogs**), Princeton (**Panthers**), Corpus Christi King (**Mustangs**), or Houston King (**Panthers**).

APPROPRIATE NICKNAMES

Some mascots are obvious matches for their schools:

Buffalo Bisons
Winters Blizzards
White Deer Bucks and Does
Crane Golden Cranes
Fort Worth Polytechnic ("Poly") Parrots
Deer Park Deer
Eagle Pass Eagles
Elkhart Elks
Farmersville Fighting Farmers
Italy Gladiators
Roma Gladiators
Hawkins Hawks
Muleshoe Mules
Panther Creek (Valera) Panthers
Veteran's Memorial (Houston) Patriots
Hamlin Pied Pipers
Tom Bean Tomcats
Van Vandals
Wolfe City Wolves

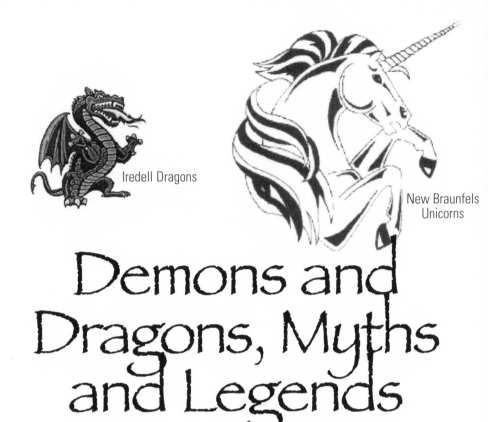

Iredell Dragons

New Braunfels
Unicorns

Demons and Dragons, Myths and Legends

It was Gen. William Tecumseh Sherman who allegedly once said, "If I owned Texas and Hell, I'd rent out Texas and live in Hell." Since William T. was not one of Texas's favorite heroes, there are a lot of Texans who said, "Amen, General, you just go right ahead." (And just to clear up any possible misimpressions, the town of Sherman north of Dallas and Sherman County in the northern Panhandle are both named for a General Sherman, all right, but he was *Sidney* Sherman, a hero of the Texas Revolution.)

However, the state does seem to be possessed by several forms of diabolical manifestations. For example, there are about a dozen dens of

Dragons (Bangs, Round Rock, Chico, Nacogdoches) scattered here and there around the place. There is only one team of **Dragon Slayers** (Bryan's St. Michael Academy), who obviously have their work cut out for them, though they could recruit some help from those **Knights** (Austin McCallum, Harker Heights, Dallas Kimball).

Bangs Dragons

80

We have our own native devils (not counting the "dust devils" that are everywhere in West Texas) and they even come in a choice of colors, **Red Devils** (Presidio, Rankin) and **Blue Devils** (Celeste, Nacogdoches Central Heights). Only Rankin is anywhere close to the Devil's River which empties into the Rio Grande above Del Rio, and none are close to the Devil's Backbone west of San Marcos. Dumas, in the Panhandle, is infested with **Demons**.

Huntington
Red Devils

There are other legendary manifestations in the state's high schools. One of the best names is **Pied Pipers** from Hamlin, based on the old German legend and the poem "The Pied Piper of Hamelin" by Robert Browning.

According to Greek mythology, the **Titans** (Longview Trinity School, Port Arthur Memorial) were the giant race that preceded humans on the earth. The **Apollos** of Houston Sharpstown honor the Greek sun god. Their logo is the divine charioteer driving his team across the heavens. Maybe Apollo's twin sister, Artemis, the moon goddess, should be the namesake of the girl's team instead of what they use, "Lady Apollos." Also from Greek mythology is the **Pegasus**, the winged horse which is the symbol of Booker T. Washington School for Performing and Visual Arts, a magnet school in Dallas.

Hamlin
Pied Pipers

Houston Sharpstown
Apollos

Port Arthur Memorial
Titans

Medieval stories told of the **Unicorn** (New Braunfels), a magical beast with a single spiral horn growing from its face. The **Griffin** was a legendary creature with the head and wings of an eagle and the body of a lion. That's the mascot of another of Dallas's magnet schools, the School for the Talented and Gifted. **Wizards** (Houston's Yes College Prep) are supposed to have mystical powers, maybe even witchcraft.

Legendary birds include the **Phoenix** (Health Careers of San Antonio, KEYS High School of Euless), which allegedly could recreate itself

81

El Paso Coronado
Thunderbirds

from its own ashes, and the **Thunderbirds**, the mythical creatures of the southwestern Indians. El Paso Coronado complains that its **Thunderbird** mascot is so unique that they have to custom-design their mascot costumes because no supplier carries it.

WERE THEY JUST FAST OR WERE THEY HIGH ON SOMETHING?

According to one story, the Dumas team was originally the Speed Demons after the fast roadsters of the 1920s. Eventually, the nickname got shortened to just **Demons**. In this day of concerns about drug abuse, Demons may be the nicer part of the original name.

GET OUT THE STAKES, FLOODLIGHTS, AND SILVER BULLETS

"Dracul" is the Romanian word for "Dragon," and "Dracula" is the "son of the Dragon." When Round Rock created a second high school, they missed their chance to name the new one "Draculas."

THEY ALL LOOK ALIKE TO US

New Braunfels got the **Unicorn** as a mascot in 1928 because they thought the Unicorn was on the Solms-Braunfels family crest. The Prince of Solms-Braunfels (a German principality) was the founder of the town. Later they found out the figure on the crest was really a rampant blue lion with one of his ears missing, so that the remaining ear looked to somebody like a unicorn's horn.

FAMOUS DRAGONS

Ty Detmer, football player (Heisman Trophy, 1990),
San Antonio Southwest

FAMOUS PEGASUSES
Norah Jones, singer, Dallas Washington

FAMOUS UNICORNS
Bob Krueger, politician (U.S. Senator and ambassador),
New Braunfels

MORE APPROPRIATE NICKNAMES

Kingsville Brahmas: The King Ranch, with headquarters at Kingsville, began experimentation with Brahma cattle from India in the early 20th century. Crossed with Shorthorns, they eventually produced a hybrid called Santa Gertrudis, which is now a recognized breed. The Santa Gertrudis cattle thrive on dry ranch land while producing good beef.

Galveston O'Connell Buccaneers: The famous pirate Jean Lafitte made Galveston Island his hideout from 1816 to 1820. He was wanted for piracy in American Louisiana, but Galveston, in Mexican Texas, was a foreign country at the time.

Houston Dobie Longhorns: J. Frank Dobie, the eminent Texas folklorist, was famous for his book, *The Longhorns*.

Santa Anna Mountaineers: The town of Santa Anna sits at the base of a large hill which is visible for miles around.

Rosenburg Terry Rangers: B.F. Terry raised a cavalry regiment in Houston at the beginning of the Civil War. Though Col. Terry was killed in action early in the war, his regiment, renamed the 8th Texas Cavalry, was always better known as "Terry's Texas Rangers."

Midland Lee Rebels: The school named for Robert E. Lee is an obvious candidate for this sometimes controversial name.

Amarillo
Golden Sandstorms

San Antonio
Sam Houston
Hurricanes

Storm Warnings

Nobody, they say, but fools and Yankees try to predict Texas weather. Good thing, too, because West Texas is full of unpredictable storms—

Floydada
Whirlwinds

the Weather Bureau can't help you here. How'd you like to be travelling across the plains and run into a **Golden Sandstorm** (Amarillo High; but most Texas sandstorms are brown) . . . or a **Cyclone** (Memphis), or a **Tornado** (Lamesa)? (Why isn't it the Tornillo Tornados? And how did Galveston Ball get named Tornados instead of Hurricanes?) Even the **Whirlwinds** (Floydada) are vicious in West Texas. And in Winters (Winters, Texas, that is) we get **Blizzards**. If you think you might have light breezes in Zephyr, think again—the town was nearly wiped out by a tornado (a real one) in 1909.

Missouri City
Hightower Hurricanes

On the coast, you naturally have to be on the watch out for **Hurricanes** (Missouri City Hightower). They even occur as far inland as San Antonio (Sam Houston).

BLIZZARDS

Winters students named the **Blizzards** in 1925, long before Dairy Queen, after a contest with several names proposed. The student who turned in the winning name later moved to Abilene and made all-state as a football guard. Dairy Queen must have been watching the town of Winters closely, since one of DQ's newer treats is a

"Breeze"—which just happens to be the name of the Winters Junior High team.

SANDSTORMS AND WHIRLWINDS

The Amarillo team is called the **Golden Sandstorm**, or just the **Sandies**. They got the name from a coach named Astyanax Saunders Douglas (with a moniker like that, he probably should not have been allowed to name anything, but maybe we're blaming him for his parents' shortcomings). While the Amarillo High baseball team was practicing on a dusty field one windy day in the spring of 1922, he yelled at them, "Come on, you golden sandstormers, come on now, bear down." The name stuck so well that Coach Douglas later formally named them at a downtown civic club meeting by sprinkling a football with sand and officially dubbing all Amarillo High teams the "Golden Sandstorm."

When Floydada played a bi-district football game against the mighty **Sandies** the following fall, they were such underdogs (they only had seventeen players) that it was said that they would only be a "Little Whirlwind" against the Golden Sandstorm. But Floydada won the game and kept the name—**Whirlwinds**.

RAISIN' A LITTLE SAND

Big Sandy (Dallardsville) and Big Sandy (Big Sandy) are both **Wildcats** and Sands (Ackerly) has **Mustangs**, while Amarillo High and Grapeland High are both called the **Sandies**. Only one coastal town comes close—the Port Lavaca **Sandcrabs**. Surely Monahans could have given the name some consideration—it's the home of the Monahans Sandhills State Park.

"SPIN-OFF" NAMES

Floydada Senior High teams are the **Whirlwinds** and their Junior High teams are the **Breezers**. The two elementary schools are the **Twisters** and the **Dusters**. It might be interesting to see a competition between Floydada (**Breezers**) and Winters (**Breezes**) Junior Highs.

APPROPRIATE NICKNAMES 3

San Antonio Theodore Roosevelt Rough Riders: Roosevelt, recently resigned as Under-Secretary of the Navy, came to San Antonio's Menger Hotel in 1898 to recruit many of the soldiers who fought under his leadership in Cuba.

Hereford Whitefaces: Because of their distinctive coloring, Hereford cattle are often known as "Whitefaces." Herefords were introduced onto the plains in the 1880s at Charley Goodnight's JA Ranch and later on the XIT, Matador, and SMS ranches. The breed beefed up (so to speak) the cattle business in Texas and "Whitefaces" supplanted the Longhorns so well that Herefords made up over three-fourths of the range cattle in the state by the mid-twentieth century.

Motley County Matadors: The school, which serves the whole county, is located in the county seat town of Matador, named for the Matador Ranch which owns much of the area.

Baytown Robert E. Lee Ganders: The Baytown Lee school was originally named Goose Creek High School and is still in the Goose Creek Independent School District.

Converse Judson
Rockets

La Rue
La Poyner
Flyers

Looking into the Heavens

Look! Up in the sky! It's a bird! It's a plane! It's . . . the **Flyers** of Larue
La Poyner and of Victoria St. Joseph. And why not? Though the Wright
brothers got lost on their way to Texas and accidentally ended up in
North Carolina, Texas has had its share of aviation history via its
numerous army, navy, and air force bases.

Or maybe what we see is something going yet higher—the **Rockets** of
Converse Judson, El Paso Irvin, San Antonio Kennedy, and Waco
Robinson plus the Wellington **Skyrockets**. Looking higher yet, one
can reach for the **Stars** at American Heritage School in Carrollton.

Perhaps one can go even beyond the stars. The church schools often
reflect their origins in the names of their teams. Though there's the
usual run of **Eagles**, **Chargers**, **Knights**, and (as previously noted)
Lions, many others among them are downright gentle. Bishop Lynch,
a Catholic school in Dallas, calls its teams the **Friars**. At least ten
schools (including All Saints Episcopal of Fort Worth, of course, and
Faith Christian of Pasadena, Waco Christian, and Dallas First Baptist
Academy) labor under what must be the heavy burden of being
Saints. An even heavier load is borne by Corpus Christi Incarnate
Word, Arlington's Burton Adventist, and El Paso's Loretto Academy.
They have to live up to being **Angels**.

ZOOM! ZOOM!

Randolph High School of Universal City has a hybrid name. When the school started in the 1960s, the proximity to Randolph Air Force Base suggested a name like "Rockets" or "Hawks." Since both of those were already taken by nearby schools, they combined them and became "**Ro-Hawks**." Their logo shows a blended rocket and hawk streaking skyward.

Universal City
Randolph
Ro-hawks

CHURCH SCHOOL CHEERS—KILL 'EM, SAINTS?

Or "stomp 'em, Angels?" And it might be interesting to listen to the competing cheers when a team from St. Joseph's of Victoria plays their counterparts from Bishop Lynch of Dallas—the **Flyers** versus the **Friars**. Or when Texas Christian School of Houston plays LaMarque Abundant Life Christian—the **Lights** vs. the **Knights**.

Dallas Bishop Lynch
Friars

MYSTERIOUS APPEARANCES

Maybe the nickname Lights should be adopted by Marfa (a.k.a. **Shorthorns**) or Anson (a.k.a. **Tigers**). Both communities are alleged to have ghostly lights that show up out of nowhere.

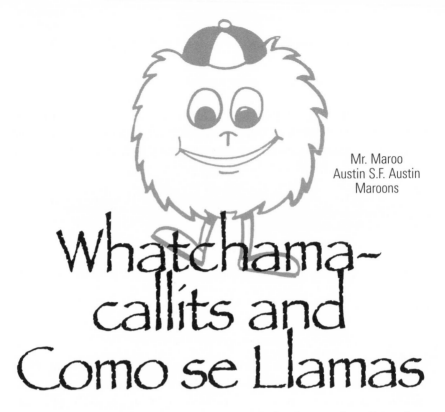

Mr. Maroo
Austin S.F. Austin
Maroons

Whatchama-
callits and
Como se Llamas

Some Texas teams have names that require further explanation, since it is not at all apparent what they mean.

For example, what's a **Provet**? That's the name given to a student at Providence High School in San Antonio—and is also the team name.

The Amarillo Palo Duro **Dons** are not mafia kingpins; the name refers to Spanish gentry.

One of the oldest team names belongs to the original Austin High School—the **Maroons.** Another school identified only by color no longer exists—the South Park **Greenies** of Beaumont.

A few highly specialized schools don't even have a mascot—such as the Houston High School for the Performing and Visual Arts, the alma mater of singer Beyonce Knowles. With no athletic teams, they feel they don't need a mascot.

Gilmer picked **Buckeyes** because they allegedly derived from pine nuts—a tough nut indeed. Apparently, they are no kin to Ohio State.

Gilmer Buckeyes

90

If the **Challengers** (Living Waters Christian of Rosenberg) beat the **Victors** (Lifestyle Christian of Conroe) do they have to exchange names? And what happens when the **Victors** play the **Conquerors** (Fort Worth Calvary Academy)? Do they both win?

The gentlest name may belong to Dallas's elite Hockaday School for girls—they are the **Daisies**.

NO SCHOOL, NO MASCOT

Two Texas counties don't even have high schools—Kenedy County in South Texas and Loving County on the New Mexico border. Forty (give or take) Texas counties have only one high school.

FAR OUT

The most isolated team is Dell City . . . the **Cougars** are 67 miles from their nearest potential prey, the Sierra Blanca **Vaqueros**. Dell City and Fort Hancock used to be in the same district but had to travel nearly 100 miles to play each other . . . and they're both in the same county. Presidio's **Blue Devils** are 61 miles from their closest competition, the Marfa **Shorthorns**.

THE BEST MERGER

Girls Lacrosse
Kni-tros

A really neat merged name comes from Austin. There's a fledgling lacrosse league around the capital city, but not all schools have enough people to play the rough sport. So, in girls' lacrosse, the McCallum Knights and the Anderson Trojans have combined to play as a single team, under the name "**Kni-Tros**."

FAMOUS MAROONS

Ben Crenshaw, golfer, Austin Stephen F. Austin, 1970
Verne Lundquist, sportscaster, Austin Stephen F. Austin, 1958
Carol Keeton Strayhorn, politician, Austin Stephen F. Austin, 1957

FAMOUS GREENIES

Woodard ("Tex") Ritter, singer, actor, Beaumont South Park, 1922

91

NAMES OF COSTUMED MASCOTS

The universities have Bevo and Reveille and Peruna. High schools have:

Lema and Leo	Greenville Lions
Louie the Lobo	Houston Chavez Lobos
Champ	Abilene Eagles
Elmo	West Columbia Roughnecks
Bruiser	Beaumont West Brook Bruins
Li'l Arlie	Arlington Colts
Stomper	Robert Lee Steers
Mighty Mac	West Hardin Oilers
Caledonia	Alamo Heights Mules
Mister Maroo	Austin S.F. Austin Maroons
Lacone Jo	Community HS of Nevada (LAvon, COpeville, NEvada, JOsephine)
Buzz	Aspermont Hornets
Geronimo	Donna Redskins
Lucky	Lockhart Lions
Buford	New Braunfels Unicorns

Fort Stockton
Prowlers

Dallas Hockaday
Daisies

Girls' Team Names

Some really strange names (and some really neat ones) are applied when you try to translate the gender of team names, especially those specifically designed for boys' teams. (The reader can decide which are strange and which are neat.)

Poteet	Agates (boys are "Aggies")
Hockaday (Dallas)	Daisies (girls only) (Hockadaisies?)
Falfurrias	Belles (boys are Jerseys)
Mason	Cowgirls (boys are "Punchers")
Porter (Brownsville)	Fighting Cowgirls (boys are "Cowboys")
White Deer	Does (boys are Bucks)
Loretto (El Paso)	Angels (no boys allowed)
Lake View (San Angelo)	Maidens (boys are "Chiefs")
Frankston, Ysleta	Maidens (boys are "Indians")
Friona	Squaws (boys are "Chieftains")
Incarnate Word (San Antonio)	Lady Shamrocks (no boys)
White Oak	Lady Necks (boys are "Roughnecks")
St Francis (San Antonio)	Skylarks (no boys)
Willowridge (Sugarland)	Wings (boys are "Eagles")
Diboll	Ladyjacks (boys are "Lumberjacks")
Harper	Lady Horns (boys are "Longhorns")

Refugio	Ladycats (boys are "Bobcats")
Bovina, Olton, Denver City	Fillies (boys are "Mustangs")
Stephenville	Honeybees (boys are "Yellowjackets")
Yorktown	Kitty Kats (boys are "Wildcats")
Tuloso-Midway	Cherokees (boys are "Warriors")
Temple	Temcats (boys are "Wildcats")
Prairie Lea	Arrows (boys are "Indians")
Moulton	Bobkittens (boys are "Bobkatz")
Kenedy	Leopards (boys are "Lions")
Comfort	Deer (boys are "Bobcats")
Fort Stockton	Prowlers (boys are "Panthers")

Most schools simply denominate their girls' teams by adding "Lady" to the team name. However, that can create some startling images. Try to imagine, for example, facing the Lady Gorillas (Trent) or the Lady Hippos (Hutto) or Lady Rockcrushers (Knippa).

Often the distinctively masculine names are transgendered for use with the female teams; for examples, consider the Lady Rams (Houston Waltrip), Lady Tomcats (Tom Bean), Lady Stallions (North Mesquite), Fightin' Lady Bucks (Alpine), Lady Bulls (Bridgeport), and Lady Toros (Laredo Cigarroa). And as for Lady Steers (Big Spring and Robert Lee, among others), don't even think about it. Thankfully, the Farwell and Graham (both Steers) both call their counterpart girls' teams Lady Blues.

Then there are the "-ettes." It's "a noun suffix, the feminine form of '-et,' occurring with the usual diminutive force, as a distinctively feminine ending." Thus saith one dictionary. Girls' teams use it frequently:

Lindsay	Knightettes (boys are "Knights")
Perryton	Rangerettes (boys are "Rangers")
Clark (San Antonio), Canyon	Cougarettes (boys are "Cougars")
Windthorst, Charlotte, Troy	Trojanettes (boys are "Trojans")
Sudan	Hornettes (boys are "Hornets")
Spearman	Lynxettes (boys are "Lynxes")

94

Robinson	Rockettes (boys are "Rockets")
Poth	Pirettes (boys are "Pirates")
North Lamar (Paris)	Pantherettes
Nazareth	Swiftettes
Munday	Mogulettes
McKinney, La Feria	Lionettes (why not Lionesses?)
Levelland	Loboettes
Brownsboro	Bearettes
Donna	Bravettes (boys are Redskins)
Bellville	Brahmanettes
East Bernard	Brahmaettes
Coahoma	Bulldogettes
Slaton, Goliad, Winnsboro	Tigerettes (Tigresses?)
Knox City	Houndettes (boys are "Greyhounds")
Samnorwood	Eagletts (boys are "Eagles")
Grapeland	Sandiettes (boys are "Sandies")
Dumas	Demonettes (boys are "Demons")
Hallettsville Sacred Heart	Indianettes (boys are Indians)

LITTLE BROTHERS AND SISTERS
(JUNIOR HIGH TEAMS)

In towns where there are junior high/middle school teams directly associated with the senior highs, the younger teams often have the same names as the senior highs—Eagles-Eagles, Tigers-Tigers, etc. In many cases, especially where two or more junior highs feed into one senior high, the names bear no relationship. But occasionally, the junior highs have imaginative names that show that they are younger siblings, names like:

Senior High	Junior High
Aspermont Hornets	Stingers
Tulia Hornets	Dobbers (as in Mud Daubers)
Bowie Jackrabbits	Cottontails
Rocksprings Angoras	Billies
Industrial (Vanderbilt) Cobras	Rattlers
Calhoun (Port Lavaca) Sandcrabs	Fiddlers
Gonzales Apaches	Papooses
Iraan Warriors	Braves
San Benito Greyhounds	Greypups
Jefferson Bulldogs	Bullpups
Donna Redskins	Three schools—Braves, Warriors, Seminoles
Seguin Matadors	Two schools—Toreadors and Fighting Toros
Harper Longhorns	Shorthorns
Tidehaven (El Maton) Tigers	Kittens
Andrews Mustangs	Colts
Sonora Broncos	Colts
Devine Warhorses	Colts (boys) and Arabians (girls)
Round Rock Dragons	Lizards (school is the old RR HS building)
Alice Coyotes (KY–yohts)	Yotes (YOH–tees)
Winters Blizzards	Breezes
Lake Worth Bullfrogs	Frogs; elementary school is Tadpoles

Round Rock
C.D. Fulkes
Middle School
Lizards

Vanderbuilt
Industrial
Jr. High
Ratters

Tuscola Jim Ned
Indians

Miami Warriors

Mascot Controversies

INDIANS, WARRIORS, BRAVES, REDSKINS, OR NONE OF THE ABOVE?

The most controversial mascots are those based on Native American culture. Critics suggest that Europeans, starting with Columbus, have never understood the indigenous peoples of the Americas. Columbus, thinking he was close to India, found what he was looking for—people with dark skins who didn't speak Spanish or Italian. So, he reasoned, they MUST be Indians.

Dozens of web sites and numerous books and articles have appeared in recent years denouncing any use of Native Americans, their customs, or their artifacts in athletic circumstances. Such usage is seen as demeaning and racist. Religious denominations, state legislatures, accrediting agencies, and other official bodies have passed resolutions denouncing the practice. There have been threats of lawsuits. The most noticeable targets are professional teams (Atlanta Braves, Washington Redskins, Cleveland Indians) and state universities (Chief Illiniwek of the University of Illinois, Florida State Seminoles, University of North Dakota Fighting Sioux, etc.), but smaller colleges and high schools have confronted the issue from time to time. In some cases, the schools have modified their use or changed altogether. As a general rule, the critics are much more vocal than the defenders of Indian mascots.

Nevertheless, many of the challenges have been ignored or deflected. Defenders of the concept see the protests as the work of a disaffected minority. They note a 2002 *Sports Illustrated* poll that concluded that 80 percent of Native Americans were not offended to any serious degree. A poll taken in 2004 by the University of Pennsylvania found that only nine percent of Native Americans were offended by the Washington Redskins theme. An opposite view comes from a 2001 poll conducted by *Indian Country Today*, a Native American group, which found that a strong majority (81 percent) of their respondents reacted negatively to such mascots.

T-R-I-B-E

Numerous Texas high schools have one form or other of Native American mascots—37 **Indians**, 33 **Warriors**, two **Braves**, two **Redskins**, two **Chiefs**, two **Comanches**, two **Apaches**, and one each of **Chieftains**, **Kiowas**, **Aztecs**, **Yeguas**, and **Thunderbirds**.

Alvarado has had some criticism of its **Warrior** mascot, with its strong Indian motif. They made, however, only minor changes, shifting their logo from an Indian head to a spear point similar to Florida State's.

Donna's **Redskins** introduced a ferocious new Indian head for its student mascot to wear, prompting objections which caused the head to be retired. Otherwise, they have received no serious criticism of their mascot choice.

Bonham has not been challenged on its **Warrior** motif, though they have a male spirit group called "the Tomahawks," a yearbook called "The Coushatta," (an East Texas tribe), a newspaper called "Smoke Signal," a Junior High using the name "Indians," and the Junior High yearbook called "The Tejas." That's the only use we have found of the state's namesake tribe.

In Jacksonville, the **Indian** teams are often called "the TRIBE," prompting an inspirational acrostic—"Toughness, Respect, Integrity, Belief, Enthusiasm."

THE ISSUE IN URBAN DISTRICTS

In the six largest cities of Texas (Houston, San Antonio, Dallas, El Paso, Austin, and Fort Worth) only three public high schools retain some kind of Indian name—Houston Lamar **Redskins**, El Paso Coronado **Thunderbirds**, and Austin Westwood **Warriors**, while El Paso has added one Indian name to the list—the El Dorado High School **Aztecs**.

Over the past twenty years, two big city high schools have changed from an Indian name. Sam Houston of San Antonio was originally called Cherokees, in keeping with their namesake's life in that tribe. However, a Cherokee came to complain about it and, after some consideration, the school agreed to drop the name and pick another by student vote, at which point the mascot became the **Hurricanes**.

The Board of the Dallas ISD decided in 1998 to "retire" Indian-related names from ten schools (at several levels) on the basis of requests from within the system, especially the American Indian Education Department. Thus, the Dallas Spruce Apaches became the Dallas Spruce **Timberwolves**.

TRIBAL PERMISSIONS

At least two Texas Panhandle mascots, the **Kiowas** of Booker and the **Comanches** of West Texas High School at Stinnett, have been officially endorsed by the respective tribes. In September 1990, Kiowa leaders visited Booker to participate in a pep rally and to cheer at the football game. At halftime, they drove a symbolic lance into the turf of the football field. One Kiowa council member autographed the yearbook with the words "Excel in whatever you do. Make the Kiowas proud."

Stinnett
West Texas
Comanches

About a decade later, Stinnett (**Rattlers**), Plemons (**Indians**) and Phillips (**Blackhawks**), merged into one school named West Texas High School. By public vote, the new mascot became **Comanches**. The district obtained permission from the tribe to use the name and tribal representatives came to Stinnett to adopt the school officially, just as had happened at Booker.

It might be noted that these endorsements do not satisfy other Native American activists. They call accommodationist tribes "Uncle Tom-Toms" or "Uncle Tomahawks."

In sum, the older schools in Texas, especially in smaller communities, have kept or added Indian mascots. In the cities and the suburbs, where most of the new high schools are being established, the issue is avoided by not giving new schools Indian nicknames.

The name **Warrior** is a special case, because it can apply to Native American mascots or to something else. In the last twenty years, nearly twenty new high schools have adopted this name, three-fourths of them private Christian institutions. Almost all the public schools with the name have an Indian motif; the church schools are much more likely to have a mascot depicting a Roman soldier.

DON'T MESS WITH TEXAS . . . MASCOTS

In Bowie, there is no mascot controversy except "every time we try to change the logo." They are **Jackrabbits** and **Lady Rabbits**.

Pittsburg's **Pirate** mascot once fell victim (briefly) to the modernization program of a new athletic director. He replaced the "Pirate" with a "Raider" and changed the school colors. A great hue and cry in the newspaper and before the school board led to a quick reversal of the changes and the athletic director soon moved on.

Celeste
Blue Devils

Questions are sometimes raised about mascots with satanic connections, such as **Red Devils** or **Demons**. Courts in other states have ruled that no religious connotations are involved and that the use of such a mascot is acceptable. Also in the religious vein, there have been challenges against the use of the word "Crusaders" on the grounds that it would be offensive to Muslims; at least one Texas college has changed its name to accommodate that concern, but a dozen high schools in the state continue to use the term.

Someone at the school once dropped the first syllable of Trent's **Gorilla** mascot, making it simply the "Rillas." A petition from the town quickly stopped use of the term, at least in print.

Poteet, a farming community south of San Antonio, adopted the name **Aggies**. Then they had to modify the hat on their mascot logo upon receiving objections from the original owners of the name at Texas A&M. (See page 61.)

A minor dispute sometimes emerges over whether they should be "Yellowjackets" or "Yellow Jackets"—one word or two? Other schools have the same problem with "Roughriders."

CONFEDERATE THEMES

In the early 1990s, Fort Worth Southwest changed its name from Rebels to **Raiders** to leave the Confederacy behind. Rebel-themed mascots are often challenged in other states, but there has been relatively little controversy over them in Texas so far.

Midland Lee Rebels

The first Austin high school south of the Colorado River was Travis and, like some other southside schools, it chose **Rebels** as its mascot from the school's beginning in 1953. Over the next thirty-five years, there were occasional criticisms of the mascot, the use of the Confederate battle flag, and the use of "Dixie" as the school song. Travis students, including African-American students, often rose up to protest the protests.

In 1989, there was a considerable fuss over this, and the decision was made to discontinue the use of the flag, since white supremacist groups had adopted it. But Travis is still the **Rebels**, and the band still plays its own arrangement of "Dixie." The character of the mascot logo has changed too, becoming more westernized. Travis uses the symbol to good advantage pedagogically. Their website announces that "the mascot, the 'Rebel,' characterizes the spirit of Travis, where we prepare students for the high tech world through innovative instructional practices, a diverse and rigorous curriculum, and a 'break the mold' attitude."

Other schools, such as Jack Hays High School of Buda, have also toned down the Confederate rhetoric, keeping the mascot but eliminating the flag. Austin's A.S. Johnston High School was named for a Confederate general killed at the battle of Shiloh. Johnston is the **Rams**, but they played the Confederate anthem "The Bonnie Blue Flag" as their fight song until just a few years ago when somebody finally twigged to what the snappy tune really meant.

Mascot disputes are usually handled in the court of public opinion, though occasionally school officials or student votes may settle the issue. Most of the time, tradition prevails: they'd rather fight than switch. Only rarely are lawsuits involved, but that may be coming. The Fifth Circuit Court of Appeals in New Orleans (which has jurisdiction over Texas, among other states) has sided with the schools and against protesters in such matters, provided only that the mascot and associated activities do not tend to promote racial segregation.

LIVE BEASTS

For years, schools with animal mascots could have a live representative of the breed available to parade around, usually at football games. Some colleges still do this, but the University Interscholastic League, which governs public high school athletic and academic competitions, passed a rule in 1979 banning them.

At the same time, the League also prohibited the use of cannons, fireworks, and other dangerous devices (paragraph 1208 of UIL Rules). These changes were made in response to a petition from the Texas High School Athletic Directors Association. The use of costumed human mascots was left to the individual school district.

Andrews
Mustangs

This move may have been purely precautionary, but there had been instances of problems with the live mascots, including excretion indiscretions. And, sometimes big or wild beasts could endanger participants and spectators. For example, soon after Andrews adopted the **Mustang** as their mascot, they were loaned a horse by a local rancher to be rid-

102

den around the field at football games. On one occasion, the horse was circling the field just as six Odessa **Broncho** cheerleaders wandered into its path. The girls were bowled over like ten-pins, but no one was seriously hurt. The pony retired back to the ranch after that.

In addition to averting potential problems, this change was beneficial to some schools. Among the mascots retired by the edict was Arlington's **Colt** mascot, "Li'l Arlie." "Li'l Arlie" ran up and down the football field accompanied by two handlers before games and after touchdowns. The white horse had green bows on mane and tail, green glitter on his hooves, and a big green double horseshoes symbol painted on his sides. He even learned, apparently on his own, to rear up at the beginning of the fight song. After the ban, the pony still put in an occasional appearance at pep rallies, which was not a violation. But for field use, the school had a special mascot costume made, an outfit that won the outstanding costume award at nearly every cheerleading camp. In 1996, the girl who wore the costume won the National Cheerleading Association's National Champion Mascot Award.

Appendix A
Alphabetical Index by Mascot

SCHOOL	MASCOT	CITY
POTEET	AGGIES	POTEET
BETHESDA	AMBASSADORS	FORT WORTH
INCARNATE WORD ACADEMY	ANGELS	CORPUS CHRISTI
LORETTO ACADEMY	ANGELS	EL PASO
BURTON ADVENTIST	ANGELS, BLUE	ARLINGTON
ROCKSPRINGS	ANGORAS	ROCKSPRINGS
ABERNATHY	ANTELOPES	ABERNATHY
POST	ANTELOPES	POST
WHITEFACE	ANTELOPES	WHITEFACE
TIVY	ANTLERS	KERRVILLE
ANTONIAN	APACHES	SAN ANTONIO
GONZALES	APACHES	GONZALES
SHARPSTOWN	APOLLOS	HOUSTON
SAN SABA	ARMADILLOS	SAN SABA
EL DORADO	AZTECS	EL PASO
BEN BOLT-PALITO BLANCO	BADGERS	BEN BOLT
BISHOP	BADGERS	BISHOP
BRUNI	BADGERS	BRUNI
BUCKHOLTS	BADGERS	BUCKHOLTS
KARNES CITY	BADGERS	KARNES CITY
LAMPASAS	BADGERS	LAMPASAS
McCAMEY	BADGERS	McCAMEY
MERKEL	BADGERS	MERKEL
ST MARYS HALL	BARONS	SAN ANTONIO

SCHOOL	MASCOT	CITY
BALLINGER	BEARCATS	BALLINGER
BECKVILLE	BEARCATS	BECKVILLE
DE LEON	BEARCATS	DE LEON
HAWLEY	BEARCATS	HAWLEY
HENRIETTA	BEARCATS	HENRIETTA
MOODY	BEARCATS	MOODY
PILOT POINT	BEARCATS	PILOT POINT
RAYMONDVILLE	BEARCATS	RAYMONDVILLE
SHERMAN	BEARCATS	SHERMAN
WHITESBORO	BEARCATS	WHITESBORO
CUSHING	BEARKATS	CUSHING
GARDEN CITY	BEARKATS	GARDEN CITY
KLEIN	BEARKATS	KLEIN
BAIRD	BEARS	BAIRD
BALMORHEA	BEARS	BALMORHEA
BASTROP	BEARS	BASTROP
BOWIE	BEARS	EL PASO
BRENTWOOD CHRISTIAN	BEARS	AUSTIN
BREWER	BEARS	FORT WORTH
BROWNSBORO	BEARS	BROWNSBORO
DEKALB	BEARS	DEKALB
GOLD-BERG	BEARS	BOWIE
LA VERNIA	BEARS	LA VERNIA
LITTLE CYPRESS-MAURICEVILLE	BEARS	ORANGE
MONTGOMERY	BEARS	MONTGOMERY
P-SJ-A SOUTH	BEARS	SAN JUAN
SAN MARCOS BAPTIST	BEARS	SAN MARCOS
THE BANFF SCHOOL	BEARS	HOUSTON
TIMPSON	BEARS	TIMPSON
URSULINE ACADEMY	BEARS	DALLAS
WEST OSO	BEARS	CORPUS CHRISTI
GLADEWATER	BEARS	GLADEWATER
SULPHUR BLUFF	BEARS	SULPHUR BLUFF
HASTINGS	BEARS, FIGHTING	ALIEF
EDISON	BEARS, GOLDEN	SAN ANTONIO
SOUTH OAK CLIFF	BEARS, GOLDEN	DALLAS
FALLS CITY	BEAVERS	FALLS CITY
FREDERICKSBURG	BILLIES, BATTLIN'	FREDERICKSBURG
SUNSET	BISON	DALLAS
BUFFALO	BISONS	BUFFALO

106

SCHOOL	MASCOT	CITY
BAY CITY	BLACKCATS	BAY CITY
MEXIA	BLACKCATS	MEXIA
LANDMARK BAPTIST	BLAZERS	MEXIA
TEMPLE CHRISTIAN	BLAZERS	DALLAS
WINTERS	BLIZZARDS	WINTERS
ST JOSEPH ACADEMY	BLOODHOUNDS	BROWNSVILLE
COLEMAN	BLUECATS	COLEMAN
NEEDVILLE	BLUEJAYS	NEEDVILLE
SNOOK	BLUEJAYS	SNOOK
BLOOMINGTON	BOBCATS	BLOOMINGTON
BLUM	BOBCATS	BLUM
BROADWAY BAPTIST	BOBCATS	HOUSTON
CELINA	BOBCATS	CELINA
CHILDRESS	BOBCATS	CHILDRESS
COMFORT	BOBCATS	COMFORT
CROSSROADS	BOBCATS	MALAKOFF
CY-FAIR (CYPRESS-FAIRBANKS)	BOBCATS	CYPRESS
DIMMITT	BOBCATS	DIMMITT
EDINBURG	BOBCATS	EDINBURG
FRUITVALE	BOBCATS	FRUITVALE
GARY	BOBCATS	GARY
HALLSVILLE	BOBCATS	HALLSVILLE
HEMPSTEAD	BOBCATS	HEMPSTEAD
HULL-DAISETTA	BOBCATS	DAISETTA
KERENS	BOBCATS	KERENS
KRUM	BOBCATS	KRUM
MEDINA	BOBCATS	MEDINA
NEW BRAUNFELS CHRISTIAN	BOBCATS	NEW BRAUNFELS
NEWCASTLE	BOBCATS	NEWCASTLE
ORANGEFIELD	BOBCATS	ORANGEFIELD
REFUGIO	BOBCATS	REFUGIO

Garland
Fighting Owls

Harlingen South
Hawks

San Antonio
Burbank
Bulldogs

Nazareth
Swifts

SCHOOL	MASCOT	CITY
RIO HONDO	BOBCATS	RIO HONDO
RULE	BOBCATS	RULE
SAN ANGELO CENTRAL	BOBCATS	SAN ANGELO
SKIDMORE-TYNAN	BOBCATS	SKIDMORE
SMYER	BOBCATS	SMYER
SOUTH SAN ANTONIO	BOBCATS	SAN ANTONIO
SUNRAY	BOBCATS	SUNRAY
MOULTON	BOBKATZ	MOULTON
FURR	BRAHMA BULLS	HOUSTON
BELLVILLE	BRAHMAS	BELLVILLE
EAST BERNARD	BRAHMAS	EAST BERNARD
HALLETTSVILLE	BRAHMAS	HALLETTSVILLE
KING	BRAHMAS	KINGSVILLE
MAC ARTHUR	BRAHMAS	SAN ANTONIO
PEWITT	BRAHMAS	OMAHA
STOCKDALE	BRAHMAS	STOCKDALE
COMMUNITY	BRAVES	NEVADA
IRAAN	BRAVES	IRAAN
BAY AREA CHRISTIAN	BRONCOS	LEAGUE CITY
BUSH, GEORGE	BRONCOS	RICHMOND
CLARENDON	BRONCOS	CLARENDON
DAYTON	BRONCOS	DAYTON
DENTON	BRONCOS	DENTON
MEADOW	BRONCOS	MEADOW
ODESSA	BRONCOS	ODESSA
SONORA	BRONCOS	SONORA
WEST BROOK	BRUINS	BEAUMONT
BRAZOSWOOD	BUCCANEERS	CLUTE
EAST CHAMBERS	BUCCANEERS	WINNIE
MILLER	BUCCANEERS	CORPUS
O'CONNELL	BUCCANEERS	GALVESTON
BRECKENRIDGE	BUCKAROOS	BRECKENRIDGE
FREER	BUCKAROOS	FREER
GILMER	BUCKEYES	GILMER
WHITE DEER	BUCKS	WHITE DEER
ALPINE	BUCKS, FIGHTING	ALPINE

SCHOOL	MASCOT	CITY
CLEMENS	BUFFALOES	SCHERTZ
CROSS PLAINS	BUFFALOES	CROSS PLAINS
FLORENCE	BUFFALOES	FLORENCE
FORSAN	BUFFALOES	FORSAN
FOX TECH	BUFFALOES	SAN ANTONIO
GIDDINGS	BUFFALOES	GIDDINGS
HALTOM	BUFFALOES	HALTOM
LONE OAK	BUFFALOES	LONE OAK
MILBY	BUFFALOES	HOUSTON
PETERSBURG	BUFFALOES	PETERSBURG
STANTON	BUFFALOES	STANTON
UTOPIA	BUFFALOES	UTOPIA
BENDING OAKS	BULLDAWGS	DALLAS
ALEXANDER	BULLDOGS	LAREDO
ALVORD	BULLDOGS	ALVORD
AMHERST	BULLDOGS	AMHERST
ANTON	BULLDOGS	ANTON
AUSTIN, SF	BULLDOGS	SUGARLAND
AVERY	BULLDOGS	AVERY
BANDERA	BULLDOGS	BANDERA
BANQUETE	BULLDOGS	BANQUETE
BARTLETT	BULLDOGS	BARTLETT
BOLING	BULLDOGS	BOLING
BORGER	BULLDOGS	BORGER
BOSQUEVILLE	BULLDOGS	WACO
BOWIE	BULLDOGS	AUSTIN
BRADY	BULLDOGS	BRADY
BROADDUS	BULLDOGS	BROADDUS
BURBANK	BULLDOGS	SAN ANTONIO
BURKBURNETT	BULLDOGS	BURKBURNETT
BURNET	BULLDOGS	BURNET
BYNUM	BULLDOGS	BYNUM
CARTHAGE	BULLDOGS	CARTHAGE
CENTERVILLE	BULLDOGS	GROVETON
CENTRAL	BULLDOGS	POLLOK
CHAPEL HILL	BULLDOGS	TYLER
CLYDE	BULLDOGS	CLYDE
COAHOMA	BULLDOGS	COAHOMA
COLMESNEIL	BULLDOGS	COLMESNEIL
COOPER	BULLDOGS	COOPER
COPPERAS COVE	BULLDOGS	COPPERAS COVE
CORRIGAN CAMDEN	BULLDOGS	CORRIGAN
CROCKETT	BULLDOGS	CROCKETT
DAWSON	BULLDOGS	DAWSON
EDEN	BULLDOGS	EDEN
EDGEWOOD	BULLDOGS	EDGEWOOD

SCHOOL	MASCOT	CITY
EUSTACE	BULLDOGS	EUSTACE
EVERMAN	BULLDOGS	EVERMAN
FLATONIA	BULLDOGS	FLATONIA
GARRISON	BULLDOGS	GARRISON
HAMILTON	BULLDOGS	HAMILTON
HITCHCOCK	BULLDOGS	HITCHCOCK
HONORS UNIVERSITY HIGH	BULLDOGS	DALLAS
HOWE	BULLDOGS	HOWE
IOLA	BULLDOGS	IOLA
IRA	BULLDOGS	IRA
JASPER	BULLDOGS	JASPER
JEFFERSON	BULLDOGS	JEFFERSON
KILGORE	BULLDOGS	KILGORE
LA PORTE	BULLDOGS	LA PORTE
LA PRYOR	BULLDOGS	LA PRYOR
LORAINE	BULLDOGS	LORAINE
LYFORD	BULLDOGS	LYFORD
MAGNOLIA	BULLDOGS	MAGNOLIA
MARION	BULLDOGS	MARION
MARLIN	BULLDOGS	MARLIN
MARSHALL, THURGOOD	BULLDOGS	MISSOURI CITY
McALLEN	BULLDOGS	McALLEN
McGREGOR	BULLDOGS	McGREGOR
MIDLAND	BULLDOGS	MIDLAND
MILES	BULLDOGS	MILES
MILFORD	BULLDOGS	MILFORD
MILLSAP	BULLDOGS	MILLSAP
MORAN	BULLDOGS	MORAN
MSGR. KELLY	BULLDOGS	BEAUMONT
MULLIN	BULLDOGS	MULLIN
NEDERLAND	BULLDOGS	NEDERLAND
NEW WAVERLY	BULLDOGS	NEW WAVERLY
NORTH	BULLDOGS	McKINNEY
NORTH DALLAS	BULLDOGS	DALLAS
NORTH ZULCH	BULLDOGS	NORTH ZULCH
ORANGE GROVE	BULLDOGS	ORANGE GROVE
PALMER	BULLDOGS	PALMER
PLAINVIEW	BULLDOGS	PLAINVIEW
PRAIRIE VALLEY	BULLDOGS	NOCONA
QUEEN CITY	BULLDOGS	QUEEN CITY
QUITMAN	BULLDOGS	QUITMAN
RANGER	BULLDOGS	RANGER
REAGAN, JH	BULLDOGS	HOUSTON
RICE	BULLDOGS	RICE
ROYSE CITY	BULLDOGS	ROYSE CITY
SOCORRO	BULLDOGS	EL PASO
SOMERSET	BULLDOGS	SOMERSET
SPUR	BULLDOGS	SPUR

110

SCHOOL	MASCOT	CITY
ST STEPHENS EPISCOPAL	BULLDOGS	HOUSTON
STAMFORD	BULLDOGS	STAMFORD
SWEENY	BULLDOGS	SWEENY
TAHOKA	BULLDOGS	TAHOKA
THORNDALE	BULLDOGS	THORNDALE
THREE RIVERS	BULLDOGS	THREE RIVERS
TRIMBLE TECH	BULLDOGS	FORT WORTH
TRIUMPH CHRISTIAN	BULLDOGS	PORTER
UNION HILL	BULLDOGS	GILMER
VENUS	BULLDOGS	VENUS
WALLER	BULLDOGS	WALLER
WORTHAM	BULLDOGS	WORTHAM
WYLIE	BULLDOGS	ABILENE
YOAKUM	BULLDOGS	YOAKUM
ZEPHYR	BULLDOGS	ZEPHYR
LAKE WORTH	BULLFROGS	FORT WORTH
BRIDGEPORT	BULLS	BRIDGEPORT
ACADEMY	BUMBLEBEES	LITTLE RIVER
CHINQUAPIN	BURRS	HIGHLAND
CENTRAL CATHOLIC	BUTTONS	SAN ANTONIO
CONNALLY	CADETS	WACO
ASCENSION ACADEMY	CARDINALS	AMARILLO
BELLAIRE	CARDINALS	BELLAIRE
BRIDGE CITY	CARDINALS	BRIDGE CITY
COLUMBUS	CARDINALS	COLUMBUS
CONCORDIA ACADEMY	CARDINALS	AUSTIN
DEL VALLE	CARDINALS	DEL VALLE
FORT WORTH CHRISTIAN	CARDINALS	FORT WORTH
HARLINGEN	CARDINALS	HARLINGEN
HERMLEIGH	CARDINALS	HERMLEIGH

McAllen
James Nikki Rowe
Warriors

Colorado City
Wolves

Texas City
Stingarees

Killeen Ellison
Eagles

SCHOOL	MASCOT	CITY
HIGH ISLAND	CARDINALS	HIGH ISLAND
MAC ARTHUR	CARDINALS	IRVING
MAUD	CARDINALS	MAUD
MELISSA	CARDINALS	MELISSA
POTTSBORO	CARDINALS	POTTSBORO
SABINE	CARDINALS	GLADEWATER
SAVOY	CARDINALS	SAVOY
SOUTHSIDE	CARDINALS	SAN ANTONIO
ST PAUL	CARDINALS	SHINER
JOHN PAUL II	CARDINALS	PLANO
LINGLEVILLE	CARDINALS	LINGLEVILLE
LA VILLA	CARDINALS, FIGHTING	LA VILLA
CORPUS CHRISTI ACADEMY	CAVALIERS	CORPUS CHRISTI
LAKE TRAVIS	CAVALIERS	AUSTIN
THE WOODLANDS - COLLEGE PARK	CAVALIERS	THE WOODLANDS
HOLY TRINITY CATHOLIC	CELTICS	TEMPLE
ST ALBANS	CENTURIONS	ARLINGTON
LIVING WATERS CHRISTIAN	CHALLENGERS	ROSENBERG
AUBREY	CHAPARRALS	AUBREY
CHRISTWAY ACADEMY	CHAPARRALS	DUNCANVILLE
VALLEY CHRISTIAN SCHOOL	CHAPARRALS	MISSION
WESTLAKE	CHAPARRALS	AUSTIN
WYATT, OD	CHAPARRALS	FORT WORTH
CENTRAL	CHARGERS	KELLER
CHRISTIAN HERITAGE	CHARGERS	SAN ANTONIO
CHURCHILL	CHARGERS	SAN ANTONIO
DALLAS CHRISTIAN	CHARGERS	MESQUITE
DUCHESNE ACADEMY	CHARGERS	HOUSTON
JESUS CHAPEL	CHARGERS	EL PASO
KEENE	CHARGERS	KEENE
SHELTON	CHARGERS	DALLAS
TRINITY	CHARGERS	MIDLAND
CROSBYTON	CHIEFS	CROSBYTON
LAKE VIEW	CHIEFS	SAN ANGELO
FRIONA	CHIEFTAINS	FRIONA
SONRISE CHRISTIAN	CHRISTIAN SUNS	SAN ANTONIO
INDUSTRIAL	COBRAS	VANDERBILT

SCHOOL	MASCOT	CITY
KEYSTONE	COBRAS	SAN ANTONIO
SOUTH GARLAND	COLONELS	GARLAND
ARLINGTON	COLTS	ARLINGTON
WORTHING	COLTS	HOUSTON
SHINER	COMANCHES	SHINER
WEST TEXAS	COMANCHES	STINNETT
CALVARY ACADEMY	CONQUERORS	FORT WORTH
DEL VALLE	CONQUISTADORS	EL PASO
ROBSTOWN	COTTONPICKERS	ROBSTOWN
ADAMS, BRYAN	COUGARS	DALLAS
AQUILLA	COUGARS	AQUILLA
BRAZOS	COUGARS	WALLIS
BUNA	COUGARS	BUNA
CALVARY CHRISTIAN ACADEMY	COUGARS	FORT WORTH
CANYON	COUGARS	NEW BRAUNFELS
CANYON CREEK CHRISTIAN	COUGARS	RICHARDSON
CHINA SPRING	COUGARS	CHINA SPRING
CHRISTIAN LIFE CENTER	COUGARS	HUMBLE
CHRISTOVAL	COUGARS	CHRISTOVAL
CINCO RANCH	COUGARS	KATY
CLARK	COUGARS	PLANO
CLARK	COUGARS	SAN ANTONIO
COLE	COUGARS	SAN ANTONIO
CONNALLY	COUGARS	AUSTIN
COOPER	COUGARS	ABILENE
COVENANT CHRISTIAN	COUGARS	COLLEYVILLE
COVENANT CHRISTIAN	COUGARS	CONROE
CROCKETT	COUGARS	AUSTIN
CROSBY	COUGARS	CROSBY
CYPRESS CREEK	COUGARS	HOUSTON
DELL CITY	COUGARS	DELL CITY
EDINBURG NORTH	COUGARS	EDINBURG
FAITH	COUGARS	VICTORIA
FORT ELLIOT	COUGARS	BRISCOE
FRANKLIN	COUGARS	EL PASO
GRACE COMMUNITY	COUGARS	TYLER
JARRELL	COUGARS	JARRELL
KEMPNER	COUGARS	SUGARLAND
KLONDIKE	COUGARS	KLONDIKE
LA MARQUE	COUGARS	LA MARQUE
LEON	COUGARS	JEWETT

SCHOOL	MASCOT	CITY
MEMORIAL HALL	COUGARS	HOUSTON
NIMITZ	COUGARS	HOUSTON
NORTHLAND CHRISTIAN	COUGARS	HOUSTON
REICHER CATHOLIC	COUGARS	WACO
ROSEBUD-LOTT	COUGARS	ROSEBUD
SAN JACINTO	COUGARS	BAYTOWN
SANTA MARIA	COUGARS	SANTA MARIA
SEGUIN, JUAN	COUGARS	ARLINGTON
THE COLONY	COUGARS	THE COLONY
TOMBALL	COUGARS	TOMBALL
VICTORY CHRISTIAN	COUGARS	BASTROP
WESTERN HILLS	COUGARS	FORT WORTH
SOUTH SAN ANTONIO WEST	COUGARS, FIGHTING	SAN ANTONIO
BRYSON	COWBOYS	BRYSON
CARTER, DAVID	COWBOYS	DALLAS
COPPELL	COWBOYS	COPPELL
COTULLA	COWBOYS	COTULLA
D'HANIS	COWBOYS	D'HANIS
EDNA	COWBOYS	EDNA
GLENVIEW CHRISTIAN	COWBOYS	FORT WORTH
GRANDFALLS-ROYALTY	COWBOYS	GRANDFALLS
HAPPY	COWBOYS	HAPPY
McCOLLUM	COWBOYS	SAN ANTONIO
McMULLEN COUNTY	COWBOYS	TILDEN
PLAINS	COWBOYS	PLAINS
PREMONT	COWBOYS	PREMONT
WOODSON	COWBOYS	WOODSON
PORTER, GLADYS	COWBOYS, FIGHTING	BROWNSVILLE
ALICE	COYOTES	ALICE
ANNA	COYOTES	ANNA
BORDEN COUNTY	COYOTES	GAIL
CARTER, JIMMY	COYOTES	LA JOYA
GERVIN	COYOTES	SAN ANTONIO

Highland
Chinquapin Burrs

Pampa Harvesters

Ballinger
Bearcats

Merkel
Badgers

SCHOOL	MASCOT	CITY
HIGGINS	COYOTES	HIGGINS
JUÁREZ-LINCOLN	COYOTES	LA JOYA
LA JOYA	COYOTES	LA JOYA
RICHLAND SPRINGS	COYOTES	RICHLAND SPRINGS
TORNILLO	COYOTES	TORNILLO
UVALDE	COYOTES	UVALDE
WICHITA FALLS	COYOTES	WICHITA FALLS
CRANE	CRANES, GOLDEN	CRANE
BALCH SPRINGS CHRISTIAN	CRUSADERS	BALCH SPRINGS
BISHOP GORMAN	CRUSADERS	TYLER
CANTERBURY EPISCOPAL	CRUSADERS	DESOTO
CONCORDIA LUTHERAN	CRUSADERS	TOMBALL
NORTHWEST ACADEMY	CRUSADERS	HOUSTON
ROUND ROCK CHRISTIAN ACADEMY	CRUSADERS	ROUND ROCK
ST ANDREWS EPISCOPAL	CRUSADERS	AUSTIN
ST JOHNS	CRUSADERS	ENNIS
ST MICHAELS ACADEMY	CRUSADERS	AUSTIN
STRAKE JESUIT	CRUSADERS	HOUSTON
SWEETWATER CHRISTIAN	CRUSADERS	HOUSTON
TYLER ST CHRISTIAN	CRUSADERS	DALLAS
BRENHAM	CUBS	BRENHAM
BROWNFIELD	CUBS	BROWNFIELD
CLIFTON	CUBS	CLIFTON
OLNEY	CUBS	OLNEY
ROUNDTOP CARMINE	CUBS	CARMINE
MEMPHIS	CYCLONES	MEMPHIS
HOCKADAY	DAISIES	DALLAS
DEER PARK	DEER	DEER PARK
DUMAS	DEMONS	DUMAS
CELESTE	DEVILS, BLUE	CELESTE
CENTRAL HEIGHTS	DEVILS, BLUE	NACOGDOCHES
PRESIDIO	DEVILS, BLUE	PRESIDIO
HUNTINGTON	DEVILS, RED	HUNTINGTON
RANKIN	DEVILS, RED	RANKIN
EL PASO SCHOOL OF EXCELLENCE	DOLPHINS	EL PASO
PALO DURO	DONS	AMARILLO

SCHOOL	MASCOT	CITY
ST MICHAEL ACADEMY	DRAGON SLAYERS	BRYAN
BANGS	DRAGONS	BANGS
CARROLL	DRAGONS	SOUTHLAKE
CHICO	DRAGONS	CHICO
COOPER	DRAGONS	THE WOODLANDS
DAWSON	DRAGONS	WELCH
INTERNATIONAL NEWCOMERS ACADEMY	DRAGONS	FORT WORTH
IREDELL	DRAGONS	IREDELL
NAGOGDOCHES	DRAGONS	NAGOGDOCHES
PADUCAH	DRAGONS	PADUCAH
REDWATER	DRAGONS	REDWATER
ROUND ROCK	DRAGONS	ROUND ROCK
SEAGOVILLE	DRAGONS	DALLAS
SHELBYVILLE	DRAGONS	SHELBYVILLE
SOUTHWEST	DRAGONS	SAN ANTONIO
TAYLOR	DUCKS	TAYLOR
ABILENE	EAGLES	ABILENE
AKINS	EAGLES	AUSTIN
ALLEN	EAGLES	ALLEN
AMBASSADORS OF CHRIST ACADEMY	EAGLES	FORT WORTH
ANDRESS	EAGLES	EL PASO
ANGELO CHRISTIAN	EAGLES	SAN ANGELO
APPLE SPRINGS	EAGLES	APPLE SPRINGS
ARGYLE	EAGLES	ARGYLE
ATASCOCITA	EAGLES	HUMBLE
AVALON	EAGLES	AVALON
BARBERS HILL	EAGLES	MONT BELVIEU
BELLEVUE	EAGLES	BELLEVUE
BENAVIDES	EAGLES	BENAVIDES
BIBLE HERITAGE	EAGLES	AMARILLO
BRACKENRIDGE	EAGLES	SAN ANTONIO
BRAZOS CHRISTIAN	EAGLES	BRYAN
BRAZOSPORT CHRISTIAN	EAGLES	LAKE JACKSON
BRENHAM CHRISTIAN	EAGLES	BRENHAM
BROCK	EAGLES	BROCK
BRUCEVILLE-EDDY	EAGLES	EDDY
CALVARY BAPTIST	EAGLES	CONROE
CANTON	EAGLES	CANTON
CANUTILLO	EAGLES	CANUTILLO
CANYON	EAGLES	CANYON
CARTER-RIVERSIDE	EAGLES	FORT WORTH
CASTLE HILLS FIRST BAPTIST	EAGLES	SAN ANTONIO
CHANNING	EAGLES	CHANNING
CHILLICOTHE	EAGLES	CHILLICOTHE
CHRISTIAN ACADEMY	EAGLES	ROWLETT

SCHOOL	MASCOT	CITY
COMO PICTON	EAGLES	COMO
CORNERSTONE CHRISTIAN	EAGLES	SAN ANTONIO
CORNERSTONE CHRISTIAN	EAGLES	WAXAHACHIE
CROWLEY	EAGLES	CROWLEY
CYPRESS CHRISTIAN	EAGLES	SPRING
CYPRESS FALLS	EAGLES	HOUSTON
DECATUR	EAGLES	DECATUR
DETROIT	EAGLES	DETROIT
DIAMOND HILL-JARVIS	EAGLES	FORT WORTH
EAGLE CHARTER	EAGLES	BEAUMONT
EAGLE PASS	EAGLES	EAGLE PASS
ECTOR	EAGLES	ECTOR
EISENHOWER	EAGLES	HOUSTON
ELDORADO	EAGLES	ELDORADO
ELLISON	EAGLES	KILLEEN
EPISCOPAL SCHOOL OF DALLAS	EAGLES	DALLAS
EVANGEL TEMPLE CHRISTIAN	EAGLES	GRAND PRAIRIE
FAIRFIELD	EAGLES	FAIRFIELD
FAITH FAMILY ACADEMY	EAGLES	DALLAS
FAITH WEST ACADEMY	EAGLES	KATY
FIRST BAPTIST ACADEMY	EAGLES	UNIVERSAL CITY
FORT BEND BAPTIST	EAGLES	SUGARLAND
GATEWAY	EAGLES	SAN ANTONIO
GEORGETOWN	EAGLES	GEORGETOWN
GOLDTHWAITE	EAGLES	GOLDTHWAITE
GOVERNMENT & LAW, MAGNET SCHOOL FOR	EAGLES	DALLAS
GRACE CHRISTIAN ACADEMY	EAGLES	HOUSTON
GRAPE CREEK	EAGLES	SAN ANGELO
GREAT HILLS CHRISTIAN	EAGLES	AUSTIN
GREENVILLE CHRISTIAN	EAGLES	GREENVILLE
HANNA	EAGLES	BROWNSVILLE
HARMONY	EAGLES	HARMONY
HEARNE	EAGLES	HEARNE
HERITAGE	EAGLES	FREDERICKSBURG
HERITAGE CHRISTIAN	EAGLES	HUNTSVILLE
HERITAGE CHRISTIAN ACADEMY	EAGLES	ROCKWALL
HILLSBORO	EAGLES	HILLSBORO
HUTCHINS	EAGLES	DALLAS
JOHNSON, LB	EAGLES	JOHNSON CITY
JONESBORO	EAGLES	JONESBORO
JUNCTION	EAGLES	JUNCTION
KOPPERL	EAGLES	KOPPERL
LAKE COUNTRY CHRISTIAN	EAGLES	FORT WORTH
LEAKEY	EAGLES	LEAKEY
LEGACY CHRISTIAN ACADEMY	EAGLES	FRISCO
LEXINGTON	EAGLES	LEXINGTON
LIFE CHRISTIAN ACADEMY	EAGLES	HOUSTON
LINDALE	EAGLES	LINDALE

SCHOOL	MASCOT	CITY
LIVING FAITH	EAGLES	DICKENSON
LIVING WORD ACADEMY	EAGLES	IRVING
LOHN	EAGLES	LOHN
LUBBOCK CHRISTIAN	EAGLES	LUBBOCK
LULING	EAGLES	LULING
METROPOLITAN CHRISTIAN	EAGLES	DALLAS
MILANO	EAGLES	MILANO
MILDRED	EAGLES	MILDRED
MISSION	EAGLES	MISSION
MORGAN	EAGLES	MORGAN
NEW CANEY	EAGLES	NEW CANEY
NEW DIANA	EAGLES	DIANA
NEW LIFE CHRISTIAN ACADEMY	EAGLES	SAN ANTONIO
NEWTON	EAGLES	NEWTON
NORTH HOUSTON BAPTIST	EAGLES	HOUSTON
O'DONNELL	EAGLES	O'DONNELL
OVILLA	EAGLES	RED OAK
PASADENA	EAGLES	PASADENA
PECOS	EAGLES	PECOS
PETTUS	EAGLES	PETTUS
PINE DRIVE CHRISTIAN	EAGLES	DICKINSON
PLAINVIEW CHRISTIAN	EAGLES	PLAINVIEW
PLEASANTON	EAGLES	PLEASANTON
PRESBYTERIAN PAN AMERICAN	EAGLES	KINGSVILLE
PRINCE OF PEACE ACADEMY	EAGLES	CARROLTON
PROSPER	EAGLES	PROSPER
RICHARDSON	EAGLES	RICHARDSON
RIO VISTA	EAGLES	RIO VISTA
ROGERS	EAGLES	ROGERS
ROOSEVELT	EAGLES	LUBBOCK
ROPES	EAGLES	ROPESVILLE
ROSEHILL CHRISTIAN	EAGLES	TOMBALL
ROWLETT	EAGLES	GARLAND
RUSK	EAGLES	RUSK
SALADO	EAGLES	SALADO
SAMNORWOOD	EAGLES	SAMNORWOOD
SAN ELIZARIO	EAGLES	SAN ELIZARIO
SANDERSON	EAGLES	SANDERSON
SANFORD-FRITCH	EAGLES	FRITCH
SCIENCE & ENGINEERING, MAGNET SCHOOL	EAGLES	DALLAS
SEAGRAVES	EAGLES	SEAGRAVES
SECOND BAPTIST	EAGLES	HOUSTON
SIDNEY	EAGLES	SIDNEY
SOUTHLAND	EAGLES	SOUTHLAND
SOUTHWEST CHRISTIAN	EAGLES	FORT WORTH
ST JOSEPH	EAGLES	BRYAN
ST THOMAS	EAGLES	HOUSTON
STACY	EAGLES	SAN ANTONIO

SCHOOL	MASCOT	CITY
STERLING CITY	EAGLES	STERLING CITY
SUMMIT CHRISTIAN	EAGLES	CEDAR PARK
TATUM	EAGLES	TATUM
TEMPLE CHRISTIAN	EAGLES	FORT WORTH
TERRELL CHRISTIAN ACADEMY	EAGLES	TERRELL
TEXOMA CHRISTIAN	EAGLES	SHERMAN
TOWN EAST	EAGLES	SAN ANTONIO
TRINITY CHRISTIAN	EAGLES	ALEDO
TRINITY CHRISTIAN	EAGLES	SAN ANTONIO
UNIVERSAL ACADEMY	EAGLES	IRVING
VALLEY MILLS	EAGLES	VALLEY MILLS
VAN HORN	EAGLES	VAN HORN
VICTORY CHRISTIAN	EAGLES	LANCASTER
WASHINGTON, BT	EAGLES	HOUSTON
WILLOWRIDGE	EAGLES	SUGARLAND
WINSTON	EAGLES	SAN ANTONIO
WINSTON	EAGLES	SAN ANTONIO
WODEN	EAGLES	WODEN
WOODSBORO	EAGLES	WOODSBORO
WOODVILLE	EAGLES	WOODVILLE
ZAVALLA	EAGLES	ZAVALLA
CHRISTIAN HERITAGE ACADEMY	EAGLES	BEAUMONT
FORT BEND BAPTIST ACADEMY	EAGLES	SUGARLAND
LAKEVIEW	EAGLES	LAKEVIEW
OAK TRAIL CHRISTIAN ACADEMY	EAGLES	GRANBURY
THREE WAY	EAGLES	MAPLE
DE SOTO	EAGLES, FIGHTING	DE SOTO
HOLLIDAY	EAGLES, FIGHTING	HOLLIDAY
SOUTH SHAVER BAPTIST	EAGLES, FIGHTING	HOUSTON
DALLAS ACADEMY	EAGLES, GOLDEN	DALLAS
KLEIN FOREST	EAGLES, GOLDEN	HOUSTON
SMILEY	EAGLES, GOLDEN	HOUSTON
OAK RIDGE	EAGLES, WAR	CONROE

Jersey Village
Falcons

Progreso
Red Ants

Alice
Coyotes

Shamrock
Fighting Irish

SCHOOL	MASCOT	CITY
DESTINY	EAGLES, WILLING	SAN ANTONIO
BURLESON	ELKS	BURLESON
COTTON CENTER	ELKS	COTTON CENTER
ELKHART	ELKS	ELKHART
EVANT	ELKS	EVANT
STRATFORD	ELKS	STRATFORD
BUSINESS & MANAGEMENT MAGNET	EXECUTIVES	DALLAS
BRAZOSPORT	EXPORTERS	FREEPORT
BISHOP DUNNE	FALCONS	DALLAS
CHANNELVIEW	FALCONS	CHANNELVIEW
CLEAR LAKE	FALCONS	HOUSTON
COUNTRY DAY	FALCONS	FORT WORTH
FAIRHILL SCHOOL	FALCONS	DALLAS
FANNINDEL	FALCONS	LADONIA
FOSTER	FALCONS	RICHMOND
FULTON ACADEMY	FALCONS	HEATH
HARGRAVE	FALCONS	HUFFMAN
HARVEST SCHOOL	FALCONS	SAN ANTONIO
JERSEY VILLAGE	FALCONS	HOUSTON
JONES, JESSE	FALCONS	HOUSTON
KINKAID	FALCONS	HOUSTON
LAKE DALLAS	FALCONS	CORINTH
LIFEGATE CHRISTIAN	FALCONS	SEGUIN
LOS FRESNOS	FALCONS	LOS FRESNOS
METRO OPPORTUNITY SCHOOL	FALCONS	FORT WORTH
MIDWAY	FALCONS	HENRIETTA
ROYAL	FALCONS	BROOKSHIRE
SMITH, A MACEO	FALCONS	DALLAS
SOUTHEAST ACADEMY	FALCONS	HOUSTON
INCARNATE WORD ACADEMY	FALCONS	HOUSTON
LEWISVILLE	FARMERS	LEWISVILLE
FARMERSVILLE	FARMERS, FIGHTING	FARMERSVILLE
LA POYNOR	FLYERS	LA RUE
ST JOSEPH	FLYERS	VICTORIA
CADDO MILLS	FOXES	CADDO MILLS
JEFFERSON	FOXES, SILVER	EL PASO
BISHOP LYNCH	FRIARS	DALLAS

APPENDIX A

SCHOOL	MASCOT	CITY
LEE	GANDERS	BAYTOWN
DICKINSON	GATORS	DICKINSON
GATEWAY SCHOOL	GATORS	ARLINGTON
ALEXANDER	GENERALS	RICHARDSON
LEE	GENERALS	HOUSTON
MAC ARTHUR	GENERALS	HOUSTON
ITALY	GLADIATORS	ITALY
ROMA	GLADIATORS	ROMA
GROESBECK	GOATS	GROESBECK
CUERO	GOBBLERS	CUERO
GRAND PRAIRIE	GOPHERS	GRAND PRAIRIE
TRENT	GORILLAS	TRENT
BOERNE	GREYHOUNDS	BOERNE
GRUVER	GREYHOUNDS	GRUVER
KNOX CITY	GREYHOUNDS	KNOX CITY
PEASTER	GREYHOUNDS	PEASTER
SAN BENITO	GREYHOUNDS	SAN BENITO
SLIDELL	GREYHOUNDS	SLIDELL
STRAWN	GREYHOUNDS	STRAWN
TAFT	GREYHOUNDS	TAFT
THROCKMORTON	GREYHOUNDS	THROCKMORTON
TALENTED AND GIFTED, MAGNET SCHOOL FOR	GRIFFIN	DALLAS
BROOK HILL SCHOOL	GUARDS	BULLARD
PAMPA	HARVESTERS	PAMPA
BIRDVILLE	HAWKS	NORTH RICHLAND HILLS
CISTERCIAN PREP	HAWKS	IRVING
HARDIN-JEFFERSON	HAWKS	SOUR LAKE
HARLINGEN SOUTH	HAWKS	HARLINGEN
HAWKINS	HAWKS	HAWKINS
HEATH	HAWKS	ROCKWALL
HEBRON	HAWKS	CARROLTON
HENDRICKSON	HAWKS	PFLUGERVILLE
HILL SCHOOL	HAWKS	FORT WORTH
IOWA PARK	HAWKS	IOWA PARK
OUR LADY OF THE HILLS	HAWKS	KERRVILLE

121

SCHOOL	MASCOT	CITY
PLEASANT GROVE	HAWKS	PLEASANT GROVE
RED OAK	HAWKS	RED OAK
WALL	HAWKS	WALL
ZAPATA	HAWKS	ZAPATA
BEL AIR	HIGHLANDERS	EL PASO
EASTERN HILLS	HIGHLANDERS	FORT WORTH
THE WOODLANDS	HIGHLANDERS	THE WOODLANDS
THE WOODLANDS - McMULLOUGH CAMPUS	HIGHLANDERS	THE WOODLANDS
HUTTO	HIPPOS	HUTTO
ASPERMONT	HORNETS	ASPERMONT
ATHENS	HORNETS	ATHENS
AZLE	HORNETS	AZLE
BLACKWELL	HORNETS	BLACKWELL
BOLES	HORNETS	QUINLAN
BYERS	HORNETS	BYERS
CALDWELL	HORNETS	CALDWELL
DODD CITY	HORNETS	DODD CITY
EAST CENTRAL	HORNETS	SAN ANTONIO
ERA	HORNETS	ERA
FLOUR BLUFF	HORNETS	CORPUS CHRISTI
GOODRICH	HORNETS	GOODRICH
GREENHILL	HORNETS	ADDISON
HARDIN	HORNETS	HARDIN
HARROLD	HORNETS	HARROLD
HEMPHILL	HORNETS	HEMPHILL
HIGHLAND	HORNETS	ROSCOE
HIGHLAND PARK	HORNETS	AMARILLO
HOLLAND	HORNETS	HOLLAND
HOOKS	HORNETS	HOOKS
HUDSON	HORNETS	LUFKIN
HUNTSVILLE	HORNETS	HUNTSVILLE
IRION COUNTY	HORNETS	MERTZON
LOMETA	HORNETS	LOMETA
LORENZO	HORNETS	LORENZO

Arlington
Juan Seguin
Cougars

Lubbock Coronado
Mustangs

Beaumont
West Brook
Bruins

San Antonio
Lanier Voks

SCHOOL	MASCOT	CITY
LOUISE	HORNETS	LOUISE
MILLER GROVE	HORNETS	CUMBY
MUENSTER	HORNETS	MUENSTER
NEW SUMMERFIELD	HORNETS	NEW SUMMERFIELD
NOVICE	HORNETS	NOVICE
ROCHELLE	HORNETS	ROCHELLE
SUDAN	HORNETS	SUDAN
TULIA	HORNETS	TULIA
WALNUT SPRINGS	HORNETS	WALNUT SPRINGS
GATESVILLE	HORNETS, FIGHTING	GATESVILLE
HIGHTOWER	HURRICANES	MISSOURI CITY
HOUSTON	HURRICANES	SAN ANTONIO
CAPTAIN CHAPIN	HUSKIES	EL PASO
HIRSCHI	HUSKIES	WICHITA FALLS
HOLMES	HUSKIES	SAN ANTONIO
ALVARADO	INDIANS	ALVARADO
AVINGER	INDIANS	AVINGER
CAMPBELL	INDIANS	CAMPBELL
CARLISLE	INDIANS	PRICE
CHEROKEE	INDIANS	CHEROKEE
CLEVELAND	INDIANS	CLEVELAND
COMANCHE	INDIANS	COMANCHE
DOUGLASS	INDIANS	DOUGLASS
FORT DAVIS	INDIANS	FORT DAVIS
FRANKSTON	INDIANS	FRANKSTON
GANADO	INDIANS	GANADO
GIDDINGS STATE	INDIANS	GIDDINGS
GRAND SALINE	INDIANS	GRAND SALINE
GROVETON	INDIANS	GROVETON
HARLANDALE	INDIANS	SAN ANTONIO
HASKELL	INDIANS	HASKELL
HUCKABAY	INDIANS	STEPHENVILLE
JIM NED	INDIANS	TUSCOLA
JOURDANTON	INDIANS	JOURDANTON
KARNACK	INDIANS	KARNACK
KELLER	INDIANS	KELLER
LIPAN	INDIANS	LIPAN
MORTON	INDIANS	MORTON
NOCONA	INDIANS	NOCONA
NORTHSIDE	INDIANS	VERNON
PAINT ROCK	INDIANS	PAINT ROCK
PORT NECHES-GROVES	INDIANS	PORT NECHES-
PRAIRIE LEA	INDIANS	PRAIRIE LEA

SCHOOL	MASCOT	CITY
QUANAH	INDIANS	QUANAH
RIESEL	INDIANS	RIESEL
SACRED HEART	INDIANS	HALLETSVILLE
SANGER	INDIANS	SANGER
SANTA FE	INDIANS	SANTA FE
SEMINOLE	INDIANS	SEMINOLE
WAXAHACHIE	INDIANS	WAXAHACHIE
YSLETA	INDIANS	EL PASO
JACKSONVILLE	INDIANS, FIGHTING	JACKSONVILLE
CATHEDRAL	IRISH	EL PASO
SHAMROCK	IRISH, FIGHTING	SHAMROCK
BOWIE	JACKRABBITS	BOWIE
FORNEY	JACKRABBITS	FORNEY
GRAFORD	JACKRABBITS	GRAFORD
RALLS	JACKRABBITS	RALLS
CENTRAL	JAGUARS	BEAUMONT
ECONOMEDES	JAGUARS	EDINBURG
EMERY	JAGUARS	HOUSTON
FLOWER MOUND	JAGUARS	FLOWER MOUND
FOREST BROOK	JAGUARS	HOUSTON
GUTHRIE	JAGUARS	GUTHRIE
HORN	JAGUARS	MESQUITE
HUBBARD	JAGUARS	HUBBARD
JASPER	JAGUARS	PLANO
JESSE JACKSON ACADEMY	JAGUARS	HOUSTON
JOHNSON, LB	JAGUARS	AUSTIN
JORDAN, BARBARA	JAGUARS	HOUSTON
MANSFIELD	JAGUARS	MANSFIELD
MOLINA	JAGUARS	DALLAS
SUMMIT	JAGUARS	ARLINGTON
CRYSTAL CITY	JAVELINAS	CRYSTAL CITY
JAYTON	JAYBIRDS	JAYTON
FALFURRIAS	JERSEYS	FALFURRIAS
KILLEEN	KANGAROOS	KILLEEN
KRESS	KANGAROOS	KRESS
WEATHERFORD	KANGAROOS	WEATHERFORD
BOOKER	KIOWAS	BOOKER

124

SCHOOL	MASCOT	CITY
1ST ASSEMBLY CHRISTIAN	KNIGHTS	SEAGOVILLE
A PLUS ACADEMY	KNIGHTS	DALLAS
ABUNDANT LIFE CHRISTIAN	KNIGHTS	LA MARQUE
BETHEL TEMPLE	KNIGHTS	EL PASO
CHRISTIAN ACADEMY	KNIGHTS	JOSHUA
CLASSICAL ACADEMY	KNIGHTS	MIDLAND
COVENANT SCHOOL	KNIGHTS	DALLAS
ELKINS	KNIGHTS	MISSOURI CITY
EPISCOPAL	KNIGHTS	BELLAIRE
FAITH ACADEMY	KNIGHTS	BELLVILLE
HANKS	KNIGHTS	EL PASO
HARKER HEIGHTS	KNIGHTS	HARKER HEIGHTS
HILL COUNTRY CHRISTIAN	KNIGHTS	KERRVILLE
HOLY CROSS	KNIGHTS	SAN ANTONIO
KIMBALL	KNIGHTS	DALLAS
LAKEWOOD PRESBYTERIAN	KNIGHTS	DALLAS
LINDSAY	KNIGHTS	LINDSAY
McCALLUM	KNIGHTS	AUSTIN
NOTRE DAME	KNIGHTS	WICHITA FALLS
RADFORD	KNIGHTS	EL PASO
REGENTS SCHOOL	KNIGHTS	AUSTIN
RYLIE ACADEMY	KNIGHTS	DALLAS
ST AUGUSTINE	KNIGHTS	LAREDO
STEELE	KNIGHTS	SCHERTZ
VANGUARD CHRISTIAN	KNIGHTS	BOERNE
WEST HOUSTON CHRISTIAN SCHOOL	KNIGHTS	HOUSTON
MARINE MILITARY ACADEMY	LEATHERNECKS	HARLINGEN
ADAMSON, WH	LEOPARDS	DALLAS
GAINESVILLE	LEOPARDS	GAINESVILLE
GOSPEL LIGHTHOUSE CHRISTIAN	LEOPARDS	DALLAS
LA GRANGE	LEOPARDS	LA GRANGE
LIBERTY EYLAU	LEOPARDS	TEXARKANA
LORENA	LEOPARDS	LORENA
NEW HOME	LEOPARDS	NEW HOME
VAN VLECK	LEOPARDS	VAN VLECK
TEXAS CHRISTIAN	LIGHTS	HOUSTON
ACADEMIC CHRISTIAN	LIONS	ARLINGTON
ALBANY	LIONS	ALBANY
ALPHA OMEGA ACADEMY	LIONS	HUNTSVILLE
BLOOMING GROVE	LIONS	BLOOMING GROVE
BROWNWOOD	LIONS	BROWNWOOD
CALVARY ACADEMY	LIONS	DENTON
CAMBRIDGE SCHOOL	LIONS	DALLAS
CASTLEBERRY	LIONS	RIVER OAKS

SCHOOL	MASCOT	CITY
CENTRAL TEXAS CHRISTIAN	LIONS	TEMPLE
CLINT	LIONS	CLINT
COMMUNITY CHRISTIAN	LIONS	ORANGE
CRANFILLS GAP	LIONS	CRANFILLS GAP
DUBLIN	LIONS	DUBLIN
EMMANUEL BAPTIST	LIONS	IRVING
ENNIS	LIONS	ENNIS
FAITH CHRISTIAN	LIONS	EL PASO
FAITH CHRISTIAN	LIONS	GRAPEVINE
FAYETTEVILLE	LIONS	FAYETTEVILLE
FRANKLIN	LIONS	FRANKLIN
GRACE PREP ACADEMY	LIONS	ARLINGTON
GRANGER	LIONS	GRANGER
GREENVILLE	LIONS	GREENVILLE
HEALTH PROFESSIONS, MAGNET SCHOOL FOR	LIONS	DALLAS
HENDERSON	LIONS	HENDERSON
KAUFMAN	LIONS	KAUFMAN
KELTON	LIONS	KELTON?
KENEDY	LIONS	KENEDY
KOUNTZE	LIONS	KOUNTZE
LA FERIA	LIONS	LA FERIA
LEANDER	LIONS	LEANDER
LEGACY OAKS CHRISTIAN	LIONS	AUSTIN
LEVERETT'S CHAPEL	LIONS	LEVERETT'S CHAPEL
LIVING STONES CHRISTIAN	LIONS	ALVIN
LIVINGSTON	LIONS	LIVINGSTON
LOCKHART	LIONS	LOCKHART
LOVELADY	LIONS	LOVELADY
LUTHERAN	LIONS	DALLAS
LUTHERAN NORTH	LIONS	HOUSTON
LYDIA PATTERSON	LIONS	EL PASO
McKINNEY	LIONS	McKINNEY
NEW BOSTON	LIONS	NEW BOSTON
NEW DEAL	LIONS	NEW DEAL
OUR LADY OF GRACE	LIONS	DALLAS
OZONA	LIONS	OZONA
PONDER	LIONS	PONDER
POPE JOHN XXIII	LIONS	KATY
PRESTONWOOD CHRISTIAN	LIONS	PLANO
RIDGEWOOD CHRISTIAN	LIONS	PORT ARTHUR
ROBY	LIONS	ROBY
ROXTON	LIONS	ROXTON
SALTILLO	LIONS	SALTILLO
SAN ANTONIO CHRISTIAN	LIONS	SAN ANTONIO
SPRING	LIONS	SPRING
ST MARKS SCHOOL OF TEXAS	LIONS	DALLAS
SUNNYBROOK CHRISTIAN	LIONS	SAN ANTONIO
TAYLOR	LIONS	ALIEF

SCHOOL	MASCOT	CITY
TEAGUE	LIONS	TEAGUE
TRINITY CHRISTIAN	LIONS	LUBBOCK
TRINITY FELLOWSHIP	LIONS	AMARILLO
TURNER	LIONS	CARROLLTON
TYLER, JOHN	LIONS	TYLER
UNION GROVE	LIONS	GLADEWATER
VERNON	LIONS	VERNON
WACO	LIONS	WACO
YATES	LIONS	HOUSTON
KINGSVILLE ACADEMY	LIONS, PRIDE OF	KINGSVILLE
CISCO	LOBOES	CISCO
CHAVEZ	LOBOS	HOUSTON
LANGHAM CREEK	LOBOS	HOUSTON
LEVELLAND	LOBOS	LEVELLAND
LITTLE ELM	LOBOS	LITTLE ELM
LONGVIEW	LOBOS	LONGVIEW
LOPEZ	LOBOS	BROWNSVILLE
MONAHANS	LOBOS	MONAHANS
MOUNTAIN VIEW	LOBOS	EL PASO
AGUA DULCE	LONGHORNS	AGUA DULCE
AXTELL	LONGHORNS	AXTELL
BRONTE	LONGHORNS	BRONTE
BUENA VISTA	LONGHORNS	IMPERIAL
CAPROCK	LONGHORNS	AMARILLO
CEDAR HILL	LONGHORNS	CEDAR HILL
DIME BOX	LONGHORNS	DIME BOX
DOBIE	LONGHORNS	HOUSTON
EARLY	LONGHORNS	EARLY
FORESTBURG	LONGHORNS	FORESTBURG
GEORGE WEST	LONGHORNS	GEORGE WEST
GORDON	LONGHORNS	GORDON
HAMSHIRE-FANNETT	LONGHORNS	HAMSHIRE
HARPER	LONGHORNS	HARPER
HART	LONGHORNS	HART

Odessa Permian
Panthers

Springtown
Porcupines

Tulia
Hornets

Greenville
Lions

SCHOOL	MASCOT	CITY
HEBBRONVILLE	LONGHORNS	HEBBRONVILLE
LAZBUDDIE	LONGHORNS	LAZBUDDIE
LOCKNEY	LONGHORNS	LOCKNEY
LOOP	LONGHORNS	LOOP
McLEOD	LONGHORNS	McLEOD
SPADE	LONGHORNS	SPADE
TARKINGTON	LONGHORNS	CLEVELAND
UNITED	LONGHORNS	LAREDO
VEGA	LONGHORNS	VEGA
WHITE,WT	LONGHORNS	DALLAS
DIBOLL	LUMBERJACKS	DIBOLL
SPEARMAN	LYNX	SPEARMAN
MARCUS	MARAUDERS	FLOWER MOUND
MADISON	MARLINS	HOUSTON
PORT ARANSAS	MARLINS	PORT ARANSAS
AUSTIN, SF	MAROONS	AUSTIN
ADRIAN	MATADORS	ADRIAN
ESTACADO	MATADORS	LUBBOCK
MOTLEY COUNTY	MATADORS	MATADOR
PARKLAND	MATADORS	EL PASO
SEGUIN	MATADORS	SEGUIN
EASTLAND	MAVERICKS	EASTLAND
MADISON	MAVERICKS	SAN ANTONIO
MARSHALL, JOHN	MAVERICKS	MARSHALL
McNEIL	MAVERICKS	AUSTIN
MEMORIAL	MAVERICKS	PASADENA
MORTON RANCH	MAVERICKS	KATY
PEARSALL	MAVERICKS	PEARSALL
MASONIC HOME	MIGHTY MITES	FT WORTH
MEMORIAL	MINUTEMEN	SAN ANTONIO
MUNDAY	MOGULS	MUNDAY
POOLVILLE	MONARCHS	POOLVILLE
SANTA ANNA	MOUNTAINEERS	SANTA ANNA
ALAMO HEIGHTS	MULES	SAN ANTONIO
MULESHOE	MULES	MULESHOE

SCHOOL	MASCOT	CITY
ALDINE	MUSTANGS	HOUSTON
ANDREWS	MUSTANGS	ANDREWS
AUSTIN, SF	MUSTANGS	HOUSTON
BENJAMIN	MUSTANGS	BENJAMIN
BOVINA	MUSTANGS	BOVINA
BRIARWOOD	MUSTANGS	HOUSTON
BROOKESMITH	MUSTANGS	BROOKESMITH
BURGES	MUSTANGS	EL PASO
BURKEVILLE	MUSTANGS	BURKEVILLE
CHISUM	MUSTANGS	PARIS
CHRIST COMMUNITY CHRISTIAN	MUSTANGS	AUSTIN
CHRISTIAN ACADEMY	MUSTANGS	McKINNEY
CITY VIEW	MUSTANGS	WICHITA FALLS
CLAUDE	MUSTANGS	CLAUDE
CORONADO	MUSTANGS	LUBBOCK
CREEKVIEW	MUSTANGS	CARROLTON
DENVER CITY	MUSTANGS	DENVER CITY
FELLOWSHIP ACADEMY	MUSTANGS	ARLINGTON
FORT HANCOCK	MUSTANGS	FORT HANCOCK
FRIENDSWOOD	MUSTANGS	FRIENDSWOOD
GRAPEVINE	MUSTANGS	GRAPEVINE
HOLY CROSS ACADEMY	MUSTANGS	AMARILLO
HOUSTON CHRISTIAN	MUSTANGS	HOUSTON
HUGHES SPRINGS	MUSTANGS	HUGHES SPRINGS
INGLESIDE	MUSTANGS	INGLESIDE
JAY, JOHN	MUSTANGS	SAN ANTONIO
JEFFERSON	MUSTANGS	SAN ANTONIO
KING	MUSTANGS	CORPUS CHRISTI
KINGWOOD	MUSTANGS	KINGWOOD
LAMAR	MUSTANGS	ROSENBERG
LUTHERAN	MUSTANGS	SAN ANTONIO
MADISONVILLE	MUSTANGS	MADISONVILLE
MANOR	MUSTANGS	MANOR
MARATHON	MUSTANGS	MARATHON
MARBLE FALLS	MUSTANGS	MARBLE FALLS
MARTIN'S MILL	MUSTANGS	BEN WHEELER
MEGARGEL	MUSTANGS	MEGARGEL
MEMORIAL	MUSTANGS	HOUSTON
MEMORIAL	MUSTANGS	McALLEN
METHODIST HOME BOYS RANCH	MUSTANGS	WACO
MIDLAND CHRISTIAN	MUSTANGS	MIDLAND
MUMFORD	MUSTANGS	MUMFORD
NATALIA	MUSTANGS	NATALIA
NIXON, JW	MUSTANGS	LAREDO
NIXON-SMILEY	MUSTANGS	NIXON
NORTH SHORE	MUSTANGS	HOUSTON
OLTON	MUSTANGS	OLTON
OVERTON	MUSTANGS	OVERTON

SCHOOL	MASCOT	CITY
PEARCE	MUSTANGS	RICHARDSON
ROOSEVELT, FD	MUSTANGS	DALLAS
SACHSE	MUSTANGS	SACHSE
SANDS	MUSTANGS	ACKERLY
SENDERO CHRISTIAN	MUSTANGS	SAN ANTONIO
SHALLOWATER	MUSTANGS	SHALLOWATER
SLOCUM	MUSTANGS	SLOCUM
SWEETWATER	MUSTANGS	SWEETWATER
TAYLOR, JAMES	MUSTANGS	KATY
WEST ORANGE-STARK	MUSTANGS	ORANGE
WESTFIELD	MUSTANGS	HOUSTON
WHEELER	MUSTANGS	WHEELER
WILSON	MUSTANGS	WILSON
PEARLAND	OILERS	PEARLAND
WEST HARDIN	OILERS	SARATOGA
ANDERSON-SHIRO	OWLS	ANDERSON
CHIRENO	OWLS	CHIRENO
COVINGTON	OWLS	COVINGTON
GARLAND	OWLS	GARLAND
HALE CENTER	OWLS	HALE CENTER
HARVEST CHRISTIAN	OWLS	FORT WORTH
HEDLEY	OWLS	HEDLEY
HIGHLANDS	OWLS	SAN ANTONIO
HONDO	OWLS	HONDO
OAKRIDGE	OWLS	ARLINGTON
ODEM	OWLS	ODEM
REAGAN COUNTY	OWLS	BIG LAKE
SILVERTON	OWLS	SILVERTON
SUCCESS HIGH SCHOOL	OWLS	FORT WORTH
UNIVERSITY PREP SCHOOL	OWLS	HARLINGEN
YANTIS	OWLS	YANTIS
JOSHUA	OWLS, FIGHTING	JOSHUA
PARKVIEW CHRISTIAN ACADEMY	PACERS	WACO

Corpus Christi
Ray Fighting Texans

Dell City
Cougars

Tom Bean
Tomcats

Hurst L.D. Bell
Blue Raiders

SCHOOL	MASCOT	CITY
PROVIDENCE CLASSICAL	PALADINS	SPRING
ABBOTT	PANTHERS	ABBOTT
ABILENE CHRISTIAN	PANTHERS	ABILENE
ALBA GOLDEN	PANTHERS	ALBA
ANAHUAC	PANTHERS	ANAHUAC
ARANSAS PASS	PANTHERS	ARANSAS PASS
BELLS	PANTHERS	BELLS
BLANCO	PANTHERS	BLANCO
BULLARD	PANTHERS	BULLARD
BURTON	PANTHERS	BURTON
CANEY CREEK	PANTHERS	CONROE
COLLEYVILLE-HERITAGE	PANTHERS	COLLEYVILLE
COMSTOCK	PANTHERS	COMSTOCK
CYPRESS SPRINGS	PANTHERS	CYPRESS
DANBURY	PANTHERS	DANBURY
DAVIS, JEFF	PANTHERS	HOUSTON
DUNCANVILLE	PANTHERS	DUNCANVILLE
EAST TEXAS CHRISTIAN	PANTHERS	TYLER
EMPOWERMENT ACADEMY	PANTHERS	AUSTIN
FOLLETT	PANTHERS	FOLLETT
FORD WH	PANTHERS	QUINLAN
FORT STOCKTON	PANTHERS	FORT STOCKTON
FOSSIL RIDGE	PANTHERS	KELLER
GORMAN	PANTHERS	GORMAN
HILLCREST	PANTHERS	DALLAS
HYDE PARK CENTRAL BAPTIST	PANTHERS	AUSTIN
KENNEDALE	PANTHERS	KENNEDALE
KING	PANTHERS	HOUSTON
KLEIN OAK	PANTHERS	SPRING
LIBERTY	PANTHERS	LIBERTY
LIBERTY HILL	PANTHERS	LIBERTY HILL
LUFKIN	PANTHERS	LUFKIN
MABANK	PANTHERS	MABANK
MART	PANTHERS	MART
MAYPEARL	PANTHERS	MAYPEARL
MEDINA VALLEY	PANTHERS	CASTROVILLE
MIDLOTHIAN	PANTHERS	MIDLOTHIAN
MIDWAY	PANTHERS	HEWITT
NAVARRO	PANTHERS	GERONIMO
NORMANGEE	PANTHERS	NORMANGEE
NORTH CROWLEY	PANTHERS	FORT WORTH
NORTH HOPKINS	PANTHERS	SULPHUR SPRINGS
NORTH LAMAR	PANTHERS	PARIS
NUECES CANYON	PANTHERS	BARKSDALE
OAKWOOD	PANTHERS	OAKWOOD
O'CONNOR, SANDRA	PANTHERS	HELOTES
OZEN	PANTHERS	BEAUMONT

SCHOOL	MASCOT	CITY
PANHANDLE	PANTHERS	PANHANDLE
PANTEGO CHRISTIAN	PANTHERS	ARLINGTON
PANTHER CREEK	PANTHERS	VALERA
PARADISE	PANTHERS	PARADISE
PASCHAL	PANTHERS	FORT WORTH
PERMIAN	PANTHERS	ODESSA
PFLUGERVILLE	PANTHERS	PFLUGERVILLE
PLANO EAST	PANTHERS	PLANO
PRINCETON	PANTHERS	PRINCETON
RICHARDS	PANTHERS	RICHARDS
SEYMOUR	PANTHERS	SEYMOUR
SPRING HILL	PANTHERS	LONGVIEW
ST JO	PANTHERS	ST JO
ST PIUS X	PANTHERS	HOUSTON
TEXAS MILITARY INSTITUTE	PANTHERS	SAN ANTONIO
UNITED SOUTH	PANTHERS	LAREDO
VAN ALSTYNE	PANTHERS	VAN ALSTYNE
WESLACO	PANTHERS	WESLACO
WESTWOOD	PANTHERS	PALESTINE
WHITHARRAL	PANTHERS	WHITHARRAL
AUSTIN	PANTHERS, GOLDEN	El PASO
POLYTECHNIC	PARROTS	FORT WORTH
JEFFERSON	PATRIOTS	DALLAS
LAKEVIEW CENTENNIAL	PATRIOTS	GARLAND
PRAIRILAND	PATRIOTS	PATTONVILLE
SAN JACINTO CHRISTIAN ACADEMY	PATRIOTS	AMARILLO
VALLEY	PATRIOTS	TURKEY
VETERANS MEMORIAL	PATRIOTS	MISSION
WASHINGTON, BT, MAGNET, PERFORMING ARTS	PEGASUS	DALLAS
HEALTH CAREERS	PHOENIX	SAN ANTONIO
KEYS HIGH SCHOOL	PHOENIX	EULESS
HAMLIN	PIED PIPERS	HAMLIN
BOSWELL	PIONEERS	FORT WORTH
HAPPY HILL	PIONEERS	GRANBURY
LUTHERAN SOUTH	PIONEERS	HOUSTON
BOWIE, JAMES	PIRATES	SIMMS
CENTER POINT	PIRATES	CENTER POINT
CHILTON	PIRATES	CHILTON
COLLINSVILLE	PIRATES	COLLINSVILLE
COOPER	PIRATES	LUBBOCK

SCHOOL	MASCOT	CITY
CRANDALL	PIRATES	CRANDALL
CRAWFORD	PIRATES	CRAWFORD
DEWEYVILLE	PIRATES	DEWEYVILLE
EULA	PIRATES	CLYDE
GRANBURY	PIRATES	GRANBURY
HIDALGO	PIRATES	HIDALGO
LA VEGA	PIRATES	WACO
LEFORS	PIRATES	LEFORS
LEGGETT	PIRATES	LEGGETT
LYTLE	PIRATES	LYTLE
MARTINSVILLE	PIRATES	MARTINSVILLE
MATHIS	PIRATES	MATHIS
NORDHEIM	PIRATES	NORDHEIM
PAINT CREEK	PIRATES	HASKELL
PERRIN-WHITT	PIRATES	PERRIN
PETROLIA	PIRATES	PETROLIA
PINE TREE	PIRATES	LONGVIEW
PITTSBURG	PIRATES	PITTSBURG
POTEET	PIRATES	MESQUITE
POTH	PIRATES	POTH
PRIDDY	PIRATES	PRIDDY
ROCKPORT-FULTON	PIRATES	ROCKPORT
SHEPHERD	PIRATES	SHEPHERD
SINTON	PIRATES	SINTON
SPURGER	PIRATES	SPURGER
VALENTINE	PIRATES	VALENTINE
VIDOR	PIRATES	VIDOR
WELLS	PIRATES	WELLS
WYLIE	PIRATES	WYLIE
MONTEREY	PLAINSMEN	LUBBOCK
ROSCOE	PLOWBOYS	ROSCOE
FROST	POLAR BEARS	FROST
SPRINGTOWN	PORCUPINES	SPRINGTOWN
MORRIS ACADEMY	PRAYING HANDS	HOUSTON
PROVIDENCE	PROVETS	SAN ANTONIO
MASON	PUNCHERS	MASON
ATLANTA	RABBITS	ATLANTA
FRISCO	RACCOONS	FRISCO

SCHOOL	MASCOT	CITY
CANYON RANDALL	RAIDERS	AMARILLO
LUMBERTON	RAIDERS	LUMBERTON
NORTH GARLAND	RAIDERS	GARLAND
NORTHBROOK	RAIDERS	HOUSTON
P-SJ-A NORTH	RAIDERS	PHARR
RANDALL	RAIDERS	AMARILLO (CANYON ISD)
REAGAN, JH	RAIDERS	AUSTIN
RICE CONSOLIDATED	RAIDERS	ALTAIR
RIDER	RAIDERS	WICHITA FALLS
RIVERA	RAIDERS	BROWNSVILLE
RYAN	RAIDERS	DENTON
SKYLINE	RAIDERS	DALLAS
SOUTHWEST	RAIDERS	FORT WORTH
STERLING	RAIDERS	HOUSTON
TAFT, WM H	RAIDERS	SAN ANTONIO
WEST RUSK	RAIDERS	NEW LONDON
LUEDERS-AVOCA	RAIDERS	AVOCA
BELL, LD	RAIDERS, BLUE	HURST
LEE	RAIDERS, RED	TYLER
WINNSBORO	RAIDERS, RED	WINNSBORO
ALLEN ACADEMY	RAMS	BRYAN
AWTY INTERNATL	RAMS	HOUSTON
BERKNER	RAMS	RICHARDSON
CYPRESS RIDGE	RAMS	HOUSTON
DEL RIO	RAMS	DEL RIO
ELSIK	RAMS	ALIEF
JOAQUIN	RAMS	JOAQUIN
JOHNSTON	RAMS	AUSTIN
MARSHALL, JOHN	RAMS	SAN ANTONIO
MAYDE CREEK	RAMS	HOUSTON
MINERAL WELLS	RAMS	MINERAL WELLS
MONTWOOD	RAMS	EL PASO
RAINBOW HILLS BAPTIST	RAMS	SAN ANTONIO
S&S CONSOLIDATED	RAMS	SADLER
WALTRIP	RAMS	HOUSTON
KASHMERE	RAMS, FIGHTING	HOUSTON
CLEMENTS	RANGERS	SUGARLAND
GREENWOOD	RANGERS	MIDLAND
JESUIT COLLEGE PREP	RANGERS	DALLAS
NAAMAN FOREST	RANGERS	GARLAND
PATTON SPRINGS	RANGERS	AFTON
PERRYTON	RANGERS	PERRYTON
RIVERSIDE	RANGERS	EL PASO

SCHOOL	MASCOT	CITY
SMITHSON VALLEY	RANGERS	SPRING BRANCH
STERLING	RANGERS	BAYTOWN
TERRY	RANGERS	ROSENBURG
TEXAS SCHOOL FOR THE DEAF	RANGERS	AUSTIN
VISTA RIDGE	RANGERS	CEDAR PARK
NAVASOTA	RATTLERS	NAVASOTA
REAGAN, R	RATTLERS	SAN ANTONIO
RIO GRANDE CITY	RATTLERS	RIO GRANDE CITY
SAN MARCOS	RATTLERS	SAN MARCOS
SHARYLAND	RATTLERS	MISSION
TOLAR	RATTLERS	TOLAR
EVADALE	REBELS	EVADALE
HAYS	REBELS	BUDA
LEE	REBELS	MIDLAND
MOUNT CARMEL	REBELS	HOUSTON
ORE CITY	REBELS	ORE CITY
RAYBURN, SAM	REBELS	IVANHOE
RICHLAND	REBELS	NORTH RICHLAND HILLS
RIVERCREST	REBELS	BOGOTA
ST JOHNS	REBELS	HOUSTON
TASCOSA	REBELS	AMARILLO
TRAVIS	REBELS	AUSTIN
WESTBURY	REBELS, ROWDY	HOUSTON
PROGRESO	RED ANTS	PROGRESO
AUSTWELL-TIVOLI	REDFISH	TIVOLI
DONNA	REDSKINS	DONNA
LAMAR	REDSKINS	HOUSTON
EL CAMPO	RICEBIRDS	EL CAMPO
WALDORF SCHOOL	ROADRUNNERS	AUSTIN
KNIPPA	ROCKCRUSHERS	KNIPPA
IRVIN	ROCKETS	EL PASO
JUDSON	ROCKETS	CONVERSE
KENNEDY, JF	ROCKETS	SAN ANTONIO
ROBINSON	ROCKETS	ROBINSON
RANDOLPH	RO-HAWKS	UNIVERSAL CITY

SCHOOL	MASCOT	CITY
ROOSEVELT, T	ROUGH RIDERS	SAN ANTONIO
SAGINAW	ROUGH RIDERS	SAGINAW
COLUMBIA	ROUGHNECKS	WEST COLUMBIA
SUNDOWN	ROUGHNECKS	SUNDOWN
WHITE OAK	ROUGHNECKS	WHITE OAK
BOYS RANCH	ROUGHRIDERS	BOYS RANCH
CENTER	ROUGHRIDERS	CENTER
ST GERARD	ROYALS	SAN ANTONIO
WEST SIDE MONASTERY	ROYALS	HOUSTON
ALL SAINTS EPISCOPAL	SAINTS	FT WORTH
BAYTOWN CHRISTIAN	SAINTS	BAYTOWN
CARROLLTON CHRISTIAN ACADEMY	SAINTS	CARROLLTON
FAITH CHRISTIAN	SAINTS	PASADENA
FIRST BAPTIST ACADEMY	SAINTS	DALLAS
HARVEST CHRISTIAN	SAINTS	PASADENA
HARVEST CHRISTIAN	SAINTS	WATAUGA
SAN JUAN DIEGO CATHOLIC	SAINTS	AUSTIN
SHADY GROVE CHRISTIAN	SAINTS	GRAND PRAIRIE
SOUTHWEST CHRISTIAN	SAINTS	HOUSTON
ST THOMAS EPISCOPAL	SAINTS	HOUSTON
WACO CHRISTIAN FELLOWSHIP	SAINTS	WACO
CALHOUN	SANDCRABS	PORT LAVACA
AMARILLO	SANDIES	AMARILLO
GRAPELAND	SANDIES	GRAPELAND
HORIZON	SCORPIONS	CLINT
SOUTH HILLS	SCORPIONS	FORT WORTH
HIGHLAND PARK	SCOTS	DALLAS
RIVIERA-KAUFER	SEAHAWKS	RIVIERA
INCARNATE WORD	SHAMROCKS, LADY	SAN ANTONIO
PALACIOS	SHARKS	PALACIOS
SABINE PASS	SHARKS	SABINE PASS
MARFA	SHORTHORNS	MARFA
SCHULENBERG	SHORTHORNS	SCHULENBERG
MESQUITE	SKEETERS	MESQUITE

136

SCHOOL	MASCOT	CITY
ST FRANCIS GIRLS ACADEMY	SKYLARKS	SAN ANTONIO
WELLINGTON	SKYROCKETS	WELLINGTON
BELIEVERS ACADEMY	SOLDIERS	SAN ANTONIO
SAMUELL	SPARTANS	DALLAS
SCARBOROUGH	SPARTANS	HOUSTON
SEVEN LAKES	SPARTANS	KATY
ST STEPHENS EPISCOPAL	SPARTANS	AUSTIN
STAFFORD	SPARTANS	STAFFORD
STRATFORD	SPARTANS	HOUSTON
TEXAS CHRISTIAN ACADEMY	SPARTANS	ARLINGTON
NORTH MESQUITE	STALLIONS	MESQUITE
SHIPTON	STALLIONS	PLANO
AMERICAN HERITAGE	STARS	CARROLTON
TEXAS CHRISTIAN	STARS	WACO
WICHITA CHRISTIAN	STARS	WICHITA FALLS
BIG SPRING	STEERS	BIG SPRING
NORTH SIDE	STEERS	VERNON
FARWELL	STEERS	FARWELL
GRAHAM	STEERS	GRAHAM
ROBERT LEE	STEERS	ROBERT LEE
TEXAS CITY	STINGAREES	TEXAS CITY
SOUTHSHORE CHRISTIAN ACADEMY	STINGRAYS	LEAGUE CITY
NAZARETH	SWIFTS	NAZARETH
GARLAND CHRISTIAN ACADEMY	SWORDSMEN	GARLAND
PORT ISABEL	TARPONS	PORT ISABEL

West Columbia
Columbia Christian
School
Warriors

Gordon
Longhorns

Fort Worth International
Newcomer Center
Dragons

Santa Anna
Mountaineers

SCHOOL	MASCOT	CITY
HOUSTON	TEXANS	ARLINGTON
NORTHWEST	TEXANS	JUSTIN
RAYBURN, SAM	TEXANS	PASADENA
WIMBERLEY	TEXANS	WIMBERLEY
RAY	TEXANS, FIGHTING	CORPUS CHRISTI
CORONADO	THUNDERBIRDS	EL PASO
WAGNER	THUNDERBIRDS	JUDSON
A & M CONSOLIDATED	TIGERS	COLLEGE STATION
ANSON	TIGERS	ANSON
ARP	TIGERS	ARP
BELTON	TIGERS	BELTON
BLAND	TIGERS	MERIT
BLANKET	TIGERS	BLANKET
BLUE RIDGE	TIGERS	BLUE RIDGE
BRACKETT	TIGERS	BRACKETVILLE
BREMOND	TIGERS	BREMOND
CARROLL, MARY	TIGERS	CORPUS CHRISTI
CENTERVILLE	TIGERS	CENTERVILLE
CLARKSVILLE	TIGERS	CLARKSVILLE
COLLINS	TIGERS	KLEIN
COMMERCE	TIGERS	COMMERCE
CONROE	TIGERS	CONROE
CORSICANA	TIGERS	CORSICANA
DAINGERFIELD	TIGERS	DAINGERFIELD
DRIPPING SPRINGS	TIGERS	DRIPPING SPRINGS
EL PASO HIGH	TIGERS	EL PASO
ELECTRA	TIGERS	ELECTRA
FLORESVILLE	TIGERS	FLORESVILLE
FRENSHIP	TIGERS	WOLFFORTH
GLEN ROSE	TIGERS	GLEN ROSE
GOLIAD	TIGERS	GOLIAD
GROOM	TIGERS	GROOM
GUNTER	TIGERS	GUNTER
GUSTINE	TIGERS	GUSTINE
HARTLEY	TIGERS	HARTLEY
HICO	TIGERS	HICO
HOUSTON	TIGERS	HOUSTON
IRVING	TIGERS	IRVING
JACKSBORO	TIGERS	JACKSBORO
KATY	TIGERS	KATY
KENNARD	TIGERS	KENNARD
KERR	TIGERS	ALIEF
LANCASTER	TIGERS	LANCASTER
LATEXO	TIGERS	LATEXO
LEONARD	TIGERS	LEONARD

SCHOOL	MASCOT	CITY
LINCOLN	TIGERS	DALLAS
LINDEN-KILDARE	TIGERS	LINDEN
MALAKOFF	TIGERS	MALAKOFF
MARTIN	TIGERS	LAREDO
MAY	TIGERS	MAY
McLEAN	TIGERS	McLEAN
MERCEDES	TIGERS	MERCEDES
MOUNT PLEASANT	TIGERS	MOUNT PLEASANT
MOUNT VERNON	TIGERS	MOUNT VERNON
NECHES	TIGERS	NECHES
OGLESBY	TIGERS	OGLESBY
ROCKDALE	TIGERS	ROCKDALE
SACRED HEART	TIGERS	MUENSTER
SAN ISIDRO	TIGERS	SAN ISIDRO
SEALY	TIGERS	SEALY
SILSBEE	TIGERS	SILSBEE
SLATON	TIGERS	SLATON
SMITHVILLE	TIGERS	SMITHVILLE
SNYDER	TIGERS	SNYDER
SPRING WOODS	TIGERS	HOUSTON
STAR	TIGERS	STAR
STONY POINT	TIGERS	ROUND ROCK
SUMMIT	TIGERS	MANSFIELD
TENAHA	TIGERS	TENAHA
TERRELL	TIGERS	TERRELL
TEXAS	TIGERS	TEXARKANA
THRALL	TIGERS	THRALL
TIDEHAVEN	TIGERS	EL MATON
TRENTON	TIGERS	TRENTON
TRINITY	TIGERS	TRINITY
TRINITY CHRISTIAN	TIGERS	CEDAR HILL
TROUP	TIGERS	TROUP
VALLEY VIEW	TIGERS	PHARR
WEST SABINE	TIGERS	PINELAND
WHARTON	TIGERS	WHARTON
WHITEWRIGHT	TIGERS	WHITEWRIGHT
WILLS POINT	TIGERS	WILLS POINT
ST AGNES	TIGERS	HOUSTON
ACCELERATED HIGH SCHOOL	TIGERS, WHITE	FORT WORTH
MERCEDES ACADEMY	TIGERS, WHITE BENGAL	MERCEDES
CEDAR PARK	TIMBERWOLVES	CEDAR PARK
SPRUCE	TIMBERWOLVES	DALLAS
CENTENNIAL	TITANS	FRISCO
IDEA ACADEMY	TITANS	DONNA

SCHOOL	MASCOT	CITY
MEMORIAL	TITANS	PORT ARTHUR
TRINITY SCHOOL OF TEXAS	TITANS	LONGVIEW
TOM BEAN	TOMCATS	TOM BEAN
TEXLINE	TORNADOES	TEXLINE
BALL	TORNADOES, GOLDEN	GALVESTON
LAMESA	TORNADOES, GOLDEN	LAMESA
GAINESVILLE STATE	TORNADOS	GAINESVILLE
CIGARROA	TOROS	LAREDO
HIGHLANDS	TRAIL BLAZERS	IRVING
AMERICAS	TRAILBLAZERS	EL PASO
TWIN LAKES CHRISTIAN	TRAILBLAZERS	CEDAR PARK
ADDISON CHRISTIAN	TROJANS	ADDISON
ALL SAINTS EPISCOPAL	TROJANS	TYLER
ANDERSON	TROJANS	AUSTIN
CALVERT	TROJANS	CALVERT
CHARLOTTE	TROJANS	CHARLOTTE
CHRIST THE KING	TROJANS	LUBBOCK
COLDSPRING-OAKHURST	TROJANS	COLDSPRING
CUMBY	TROJANS	CUMBY
HEALEY-MURPHY	TROJANS	SAN ANTONIO
JONES, A C	TROJANS	BEEVILLE
MADISON	TROJANS	DALLAS
MOODY	TROJANS	CORPUS CHRISTI
SAN PERLITA	TROJANS	SAN PERLITA
SMITH, NEWMAN	TROJANS	CARROLLTON
SOUTH HOUSTON	TROJANS	HOUSTON
TRINIDAD	TROJANS	TRINIDAD
TRINITY	TROJANS	EULESS
TRINITY CHRISTIAN ACADEMY	TROJANS	ADDISON
TRINITY VALLEY	TROJANS	FORT WORTH
TROY	TROJANS	TROY
UNIVERSITY	TROJANS	WACO
WEST	TROJANS	WEST
WINDTHORST	TROJANS	WINDTHORST
EASTWOOD	TROOPERS	EL PASO
NEW BRAUNFELS	UNICORNS	NEW BRAUNFELS
SELWYN SCHOOL	UNICORNS	DENTON
VAN	VANDALS	VAN

SCHOOL	MASCOT	CITY
SAN DIEGO	VAQUEROS	SAN DIEGO
SIERRA BLANCA	VAQUEROS	SIERRA BLANCA
LIFESTYLE CHRISTIAN	VICTORS	CONROE
BRYAN	VIKINGS	BRYAN
DULLES	VIKINGS	SUGARLAND
LAGO VISTA	VIKINGS	LAGO VISTA
LAMAR	VIKINGS	ARLINGTON
LANIER	VIKINGS	AUSTIN
NIMITZ	VIKINGS	IRVING
NOLAN CATHOLIC	VIKINGS	FORT WORTH
PACE	VIKINGS	BROWNSVILLE
PINKSTON	VIKINGS	DALLAS
VANGUARD	VIKINGS	WACO
VINES	VIKINGS	PLANO
MEMORIAL	VIPERS	VICTORIA
LANIER	VOKS	SAN ANTONIO
BOWIE	VOLUNTEERS	ARLINGTON
LEE	VOLUNTEERS	SAN ANTONIO
ITASCA	WAMPUS CATS	ITASCA
DEVINE	WARHORSES	DEVINE
CATHEDRAL CHRISTIAN	WARRIORS	BEAUMONT
CHANNELVIEW CHRISTIAN	WARRIORS	CHANNELVIEW
CHRISTIAN ACADEMY	WARRIORS	LUCAS
CHRISTIAN ACADEMY	WARRIORS	THE WOODLANDS
CHRISTIAN LIFE FELLOWSHIP	WARRIORS	SEVEN POINTS
COLUMBIA CHRISTIAN	WARRIORS	WEST COLUMBIA
COMMUNITY CHRISTIAN	WARRIORS	CYPRESS
FAMILY CHRISTIAN	WARRIORS	HOUSTON
FARMERSVILLE CHRISTIAN ACADEMY	WARRIORS	FARMERSVILLE
FIRST BAPTIST	WARRIORS	PASADENA
HIGHLAND AVENUE	WARRIORS	ARANSAS PASS
HONEY GROVE	WARRIORS	HONEY GROVE
LAKEHILL PREP	WARRIORS	DALLAS
LIBERTY CHRISTIAN	WARRIORS	LIBERTY
LIVINGWAY CHRISTIAN	WARRIORS	BROWNSVILLE
MARTIN	WARRIORS	ARLINGTON
MIAMI	WARRIORS	MIAMI
MOORE,TOM	WARRIORS	INGRAM
NORTHEAST CHRISTIAN ACADEMY	WARRIORS	KINGWOOD
ROCKWALL CHRISTIAN	WARRIORS	ROWLETT

SCHOOL	MASCOT	CITY
ROWE	WARRIORS	McALLEN
SANTA ROSA	WARRIORS	SANTA ROSA
SOUTH GRAND PRAIRIE	WARRIORS	GRAND PRAIRIE
TULOSO-MIDWAY	WARRIORS	CORPUS CHRISTI
WACO CHRISTIAN FELLOWSHIP	WARRIORS	WACO
WARREN	WARRIORS	SAN ANTONIO
WARREN	WARRIORS	WARREN
WESTWOOD	WARRIORS	AUSTIN
WILLIAMS	WARRIORS	PLANO
WOODLANDS CHRISTIAN	WARRIORS	CONROE
BRACKEN CHRISTIAN	WARRIORS	BULVERDE
ENCOURAGER CHRISTIAN	WARRIORS, MIGHTY	HOUSTON
BONHAM	WARRIORS, PURPLE	BONHAM
TEMPLE CHRISTIAN	WATCHMEN	LEWISVILLE
LUBBOCK	WESTERNERS	LUBBOCK
FLOYDADA	WHIRLWINDS	FLOYDADA
HEREFORD	WHITEFACES	HEREFORD
ANGLETON	WILDCATS	ANGLETON
ANTHONY	WILDCATS	ANTHONY
ARCHER CITY	WILDCATS	ARCHER CITY
BIG SANDY	WILDCATS	BIG SANDY
BIG SANDY	WILDCATS	DALLARDSVILLE
BLOOMBURG	WILDCATS	BLOOMBURG
BROOKLAND	WILDCATS	BROOKLAND
CALALLEN	WILDCATS	CORPUS CHRISTI
CALLISBURG	WILDCATS	GAINESVILLE
CANADIAN	WILDCATS	CANADIAN
CARRIZO SPRINGS	WILDCATS	CARRIZO SPRINGS
CAYUGA	WILDCATS	CAYUGA
CLEAR CREEK	WILDCATS	LEAGUE CITY
CROWELL	WILDCATS	CROWELL
ELGIN	WILDCATS	ELGIN
FABENS	WILDCATS	FABENS
GODLEY	WILDCATS	GODLEY
GRADY	WILDCATS	LENORAH
GREGORY-PORTLAND	WILDCATS	PORTLAND
GUYER	WILDCATS	DENTON
HARLETON	WILDCATS	HARLETON
HUMBLE	WILDCATS	HUMBLE
IDALOU	WILDCATS	IDALOU
KIRBYVILLE	WILDCATS	KIRBYVILLE

142

SCHOOL	MASCOT	CITY
LAKE HIGHLANDS	WILDCATS	DALLAS
LITTLEFIELD	WILDCATS	LITTLEFIELD
MOUNT ENTERPRISE	WILDCATS	MOUNT ENTERPRISE
ONALASKA	WILDCATS	ONALASKA
PALESTINE	WILDCATS	PALESTINE
PARIS	WILDCATS	PARIS
PLANO	WILDCATS	PLANO
RAINS	WILDCATS	RAINS
RISING STAR	WILDCATS	RISING STAR
RIVER ROAD	WILDCATS	AMARILLO
SANTO	WILDCATS	SANTO
SCURRY-ROSSER	WILDCATS	SCURRY
SPLENDORA	WILDCATS	SPLENDORA
SULPHUR SPRINGS	WILDCATS	SULPHUR SPRINGS
TEMPLE	WILDCATS	TEMPLE
TEXAS SCHOOL FOR THE BLIND	WILDCATS	AUSTIN
WAELDER	WILDCATS	WAELDER
WASKOM	WILDCATS	WASKOM
WATER VALLEY	WILDCATS	WATER VALLEY
WEIMAR	WILDCATS	WEIMAR
WELLMAN UNION	WILDCATS	WELLMAN
WESLACO EAST	WILDCATS	WESLACO
WESTBROOK	WILDCATS	WESTBROOK
WESTBURY CHRISTIAN	WILDCATS	HOUSTON
WHEATLEY, P	WILDCATS	HOUSTON
WHITEHOUSE	WILDCATS	WHITEHOUSE
WHITNEY	WILDCATS	WHITNEY
WILSON, WOODROW	WILDCATS	DALLAS
WINK	WILDCATS	WINK
WINONA	WILDCATS	WINONA
YORKTOWN	WILDCATS	YORKTOWN
DUNBAR	WILDCATS, FIGHTIN'	FORT WORTH
WILLIS	WILDKATS	WILLIS
NEY	WIZARDS	NEW BRAUNFELS
YES COLLEGE PREP	WIZARDS	HOUSTON
CLEAR BROOK	WOLVERINES	FRIENDSWOOD
MEMORIAL	WOLVERINES	ALAMO
PENELOPE	WOLVERINES	PENELOPE
SPRINGLAKE-EARTH	WOLVERINES	EARTH
COLORADO CITY	WOLVES	COLORADO CITY
DILLEY	WOLVES	DILLEY
JOHNSON, LB	WOLVES	LAREDO
PLANO WEST	WOLVES	PLANO

SCHOOL	MASCOT	CITY
RANCHVIEW	WOLVES	IRVING
SAN AUGUSTINE	WOLVES	SAN AUGUSTINE
SCHOOL OF EXCELLENCE	WOLVES	SAN ANTONIO
TIMBERVIEW	WOLVES	MANSFIELD
WESTSIDE	WOLVES	HOUSTON
WOLFE CITY	WOLVES	WOLFE CITY
DALHART	WOLVES, GOLDEN	DALHART
SHOEMAKER	WOLVES, GREY	KILLEEN
WEST MESQUITE	WRANGLERS	MESQUITE
SOMERVILLE	YEGUAS	SOMERVILLE
ROTAN	YELLOWHAMMERS	ROTAN
ALTO	YELLOWJACKETS	ALTO
ALVIN	YELLOWJACKETS	ALVIN
ARLINGTON HEIGHTS	YELLOWJACKETS	FORT WORTH
BOYD	YELLOWJACKETS	BOYD
CHESTER	YELLOWJACKETS	CHESTER
CLEBURNE	YELLOWJACKETS	CLEBURNE
COOLIDGE	YELLOWJACKETS	COOLIDGE
DENISON	YELLOWJACKETS	DENISON
EDCOUCH-ELSA	YELLOWJACKETS	EDCOUCH
ELYSIAN FIELDS	YELLOWJACKETS	ELYSIAN FIELDS
FERRIS	YELLOWJACKETS	FERRIS
GALENA PARK	YELLOWJACKETS	GALENA PARK
KEMP	YELLOWJACKETS	KEMP
KERMIT	YELLOWJACKETS	KERMIT
LANEVILLE	YELLOWJACKETS	LANEVILLE
LLANO	YELLOWJACKETS	LLANO
MENARD	YELLOWJACKETS	MENARD
MERIDIAN	YELLOWJACKETS	MERIDIAN
MINEOLA	YELLOWJACKETS	MINEOLA
ROCKWALL	YELLOWJACKETS	ROCKWALL
RUNGE	YELLOWJACKETS	RUNGE
SABINAL	YELLOWJACKETS	SABINAL
ST ANTHONY CATHOLIC	YELLOWJACKETS	SAN ANTONIO
STEPHENVILLE	YELLOWJACKETS	STEPHENVILLE
YOE	YOEMEN	CAMERON
GRANDVIEW	ZEBRAS	GRANDVIEW

Appendix B
Alphabetical Index by School

SCHOOL	MASCOT	CITY
1ST ASSEMBLY CHRISTIAN	KNIGHTS	SEAGOVILLE
A & M CONSOLIDATED	TIGERS	COLLEGE STATION
A PLUS ACADEMY	KNIGHTS	DALLAS
ABBOTT	PANTHERS	ABBOTT
ABERNATHY	ANTELOPES	ABERNATHY
ABILENE	EAGLES	ABILENE
ABILENE CHRISTIAN	PANTHERS	ABILENE
ABUNDANT LIFE CHRISTIAN	KNIGHTS	LA MARQUE
ACADEMIC CHRISTIAN	LIONS	ARLINGTON
ACADEMY	BUMBLEBEES	LITTLE RIVER
ACCELERATED HIGH SCHOOL	TIGERS, WHITE	FORT WORTH
ADAMS, BRYAN	COUGARS	DALLAS
ADAMSON, WH	LEOPARDS	DALLAS
ADDISON CHRISTIAN	TROJANS	ADDISON
ADRIAN	MATADORS	ADRIAN
AGUA DULCE	LONGHORNS	AGUA DULCE
AKINS	EAGLES	AUSTIN
ALAMO HEIGHTS	MULES	SAN ANTONIO
ALBA GOLDEN	PANTHERS	ALBA
ALBANY	LIONS	ALBANY
ALDINE	MUSTANGS	HOUSTON
ALEXANDER	BULLDOGS	LAREDO
ALEXANDER	GENERALS	RICHARDSON
ALICE	COYOTES	ALICE
ALL SAINTS EPISCOPAL	SAINTS	FT WORTH
ALL SAINTS EPISCOPAL	TROJANS	TYLER
ALLEN	EAGLES	ALLEN
ALLEN ACADEMY	RAMS	BRYAN
ALPHA OMEGA ACADEMY	LIONS	HUNTSVILLE
ALPINE	BUCKS, FIGHTING	ALPINE
ALTO	YELLOWJACKETS	ALTO
ALVARADO	INDIANS	ALVARADO
ALVIN	YELLOWJACKETS	ALVIN
ALVORD	BULLDOGS	ALVORD
AMARILLO	SANDIES	AMARILLO
AMBASSADORS OF CHRIST ACADEMY	EAGLES	FORT WORTH
AMERICAN HERITAGE	STARS	CARROLTON
AMERICAS	TRAILBLAZERS	EL PASO
AMHERST	BULLDOGS	AMHERST

SCHOOL	MASCOT	CITY
ANAHUAC	PANTHERS	ANAHUAC
ANDERSON	TROJANS	AUSTIN
ANDERSON-SHIRO	OWLS	ANDERSON
ANDRESS	EAGLES	EL PASO
ANDREWS	MUSTANGS	ANDREWS
ANGELO CHRISTIAN	EAGLES	SAN ANGELO
ANGLETON	WILDCATS	ANGLETON
ANNA	COYOTES	ANNA
ANSON	TIGERS	ANSON
ANTHONY	WILDCATS	ANTHONY
ANTON	BULLDOGS	ANTON
ANTONIAN	APACHES	SAN ANTONIO
APPLE SPRINGS	EAGLES	APPLE SPRINGS
AQUILLA	COUGARS	AQUILLA
ARANSAS PASS	PANTHERS	ARANSAS PASS
ARCHER CITY	WILDCATS	ARCHER CITY
ARGYLE	EAGLES	ARGYLE
ARLINGTON	COLTS	ARLINGTON
ARLINGTON HEIGHTS	YELLOWJACKETS	FORT WORTH
ARP	TIGERS	ARP
ASCENSION ACADEMY	CARDINALS	AMARILLO
ASPERMONT	HORNETS	ASPERMONT
ATASCOCITA	EAGLES	HUMBLE
ATHENS	HORNETS	ATHENS
ATLANTA	RABBITS	ATLANTA
AUBREY	CHAPARRALS	AUBREY
AUSTIN	PANTHERS, GOLDEN	EI PASO
AUSTIN, SF	BULLDOGS	SUGARLAND
AUSTIN, SF	MAROONS	AUSTIN
AUSTIN, SF	MUSTANGS	HOUSTON
AUSTWELL-TIVOLI	REDFISH	TIVOLI
AVALON	EAGLES	AVALON
AVERY	BULLDOGS	AVERY
AVINGER	INDIANS	AVINGER
AWTY INTERNATL	RAMS	HOUSTON
AXTELL	LONGHORNS	AXTELL
AZLE	HORNETS	AZLE
BAIRD	BEARS	BAIRD
BALCH SPRINGS CHRISTIAN	CRUSADERS	BALCH SPRINGS
BALL	TORNADOES, GOLDEN	GALVESTON
BALLINGER	BEARCATS	BALLINGER
BALMORHEA	BEARS	BALMORHEA
BANDERA	BULLDOGS	BANDERA
BANGS	DRAGONS	BANGS
BANQUETE	BULLDOGS	BANQUETE
BARBERS HILL	EAGLES	MONT BELVIEU
BARTLETT	BULLDOGS	BARTLETT

SCHOOL	MASCOT	CITY
BASTROP	BEARS	BASTROP
BAY AREA CHRISTIAN	BRONCOS	LEAGUE CITY
BAY CITY	BLACKCATS	BAY CITY
BAYTOWN CHRISTIAN	SAINTS	BAYTOWN
BECKVILLE	BEARCATS	BECKVILLE
BEL AIR	HIGHLANDERS	EL PASO
BELIEVERS ACADEMY	SOLDIERS	SAN ANTONIO
BELL, LD	RAIDERS, BLUE	HURST
BELLAIRE	CARDINALS	BELLAIRE
BELLEVUE	EAGLES	BELLEVUE
BELLS	PANTHERS	BELLS
BELLVILLE	BRAHMAS	BELLVILLE
BELTON	TIGERS	BELTON
BEN BOLT-PALITO BLANCO	BADGERS	BEN BOLT
BENAVIDES	EAGLES	BENAVIDES
BENDING OAKS	BULLDAWGS	DALLAS
BENJAMIN	MUSTANGS	BENJAMIN
BERKNER	RAMS	RICHARDSON
BETHEL TEMPLE	KNIGHTS	EL PASO
BETHESDA	AMBASSADORS	FORT WORTH
BIBLE HERITAGE	EAGLES	AMARILLO
BIG SANDY	WILDCATS	BIG SANDY
BIG SANDY	WILDCATS	DALLARDSVILLE
BIG SPRING	STEERS	BIG SPRING
BIRDVILLE	HAWKS	NORTH RICHLAND HILLS
BISHOP	BADGERS	BISHOP
BISHOP DUNNE	FALCONS	DALLAS
BISHOP GORMAN	CRUSADERS	TYLER
BISHOP LYNCH	FRIARS	DALLAS
BLACKWELL	HORNETS	BLACKWELL
BLANCO	PANTHERS	BLANCO
BLAND	TIGERS	MERIT
BLANKET	TIGERS	BLANKET
BLOOMBURG	WILDCATS	BLOOMBURG
BLOOMING GROVE	LIONS	BLOOMING GROVE
BLOOMINGTON	BOBCATS	BLOOMINGTON

Galveston Ball
Tornadoes

White Oak
Roughnecks

Robert Lee
Steers

Poolville
Monarchs

SCHOOL	MASCOT	CITY
BLUE RIDGE	TIGERS	BLUE RIDGE
BLUM	BOBCATS	BLUM
BOERNE	GREYHOUNDS	BOERNE
BOLES	HORNETS	QUINLAN
BOLING	BULLDOGS	BOLING
BONHAM	WARRIORS, PURPLE	BONHAM
BOOKER	KIOWAS	BOOKER
BORDEN COUNTY	COYOTES	GAIL
BORGER	BULLDOGS	BORGER
BOSQUEVILLE	BULLDOGS	WACO
BOSWELL	PIONEERS	FORT WORTH
BOVINA	MUSTANGS	BOVINA
BOWIE	JACKRABBITS	BOWIE
BOWIE	BEARS	EL PASO
BOWIE	BULLDOGS	AUSTIN
BOWIE	VOLUNTEERS	ARLINGTON
BOWIE, JAMES	PIRATES	SIMMS
BOYD	YELLOWJACKETS	BOYD
BOYS RANCH	ROUGHRIDERS	BOYS RANCH
BRACKEN CHRISTIAN	WARRIORS	BULVERDE
BRACKENRIDGE	EAGLES	SAN ANTONIO
BRACKETT	TIGERS	BRACKETVILLE
BRADY	BULLDOGS	BRADY
BRAZOS	COUGARS	WALLIS
BRAZOS CHRISTIAN	EAGLES	BRYAN
BRAZOSPORT	EXPORTERS	FREEPORT
BRAZOSPORT CHRISTIAN	EAGLES	LAKE JACKSON
BRAZOSWOOD	BUCCANEERS	CLUTE
BRECKENRIDGE	BUCKAROOS	BRECKENRIDGE
BREMOND	TIGERS	BREMOND
BRENHAM	CUBS	BRENHAM
BRENHAM CHRISTIAN	EAGLES	BRENHAM
BRENTWOOD CHRISTIAN	BEARS	AUSTIN
BREWER	BEARS	FORT WORTH
BRIARWOOD	MUSTANGS	HOUSTON
BRIDGE CITY	CARDINALS	BRIDGE CITY
BRIDGEPORT	BULLS	BRIDGEPORT
BROADDUS	BULLDOGS	BROADDUS
BROADWAY BAPTIST	BOBCATS	HOUSTON
BROCK	EAGLES	BROCK
BRONTE	LONGHORNS	BRONTE
BROOK HILL SCHOOL	GUARDS	BULLARD
BROOKESMITH	MUSTANGS	BROOKESMITH
BROOKLAND	WILDCATS	BROOKLAND
BROWNFIELD	CUBS	BROWNFIELD
BROWNSBORO	BEARS	BROWNSBORO
BROWNWOOD	LIONS	BROWNWOOD
BRUCEVILLE-EDDY	EAGLES	EDDY

SCHOOL	MASCOT	CITY
BRUNI	BADGERS	BRUNI
BRYAN	VIKINGS	BRYAN
BRYSON	COWBOYS	BRYSON
BUCKHOLTS	BADGERS	BUCKHOLTS
BUENA VISTA	LONGHORNS	IMPERIAL
BUFFALO	BISONS	BUFFALO
BULLARD	PANTHERS	BULLARD
BUNA	COUGARS	BUNA
BURBANK	BULLDOGS	SAN ANTONIO
BURGES	MUSTANGS	EL PASO
BURKBURNETT	BULLDOGS	BURKBURNETT
BURKEVILLE	MUSTANGS	BURKEVILLE
BURLESON	ELKS	BURLESON
BURNET	BULLDOGS	BURNET
BURTON	PANTHERS	BURTON
BURTON ADVENTIST	ANGELS, BLUE	ARLINGTON
BUSH, GEORGE	BRONCOS	RICHMOND
BUSINESS & MANAGEMENT MAGNET	EXECUTIVES	DALLAS
BYERS	HORNETS	BYERS
BYNUM	BULLDOGS	BYNUM
CADDO MILLS	FOXES	CADDO MILLS
CALALLEN	WILDCATS	CORPUS CHRISTI
CALDWELL	HORNETS	CALDWELL
CALHOUN	SANDCRABS	PORT LAVACA
CALLISBURG	WILDCATS	GAINESVILLE
CALVARY ACADEMY	CONQUERORS	FORT WORTH
CALVARY ACADEMY	LIONS	DENTON
CALVARY BAPTIST	EAGLES	CONROE
CALVARY CHRISTIAN ACADEMY	COUGARS	FORT WORTH
CALVERT	TROJANS	CALVERT
CAMBRIDGE SCHOOL	LIONS	DALLAS
CAMPBELL	INDIANS	CAMPBELL
CANADIAN	WILDCATS	CANADIAN
CANEY CREEK	PANTHERS	CONROE
CANTERBURY EPISCOPAL	CRUSADERS	DESOTO
CANTON	EAGLES	CANTON
CANUTILLO	EAGLES	CANUTILLO
CANYON	EAGLES	CANYON
CANYON	COUGARS	NEW BRAUNFELS
CANYON CREEK CHRISTIAN	COUGARS	RICHARDSON
CANYON RANDALL	RAIDERS	AMARILLO
CAPROCK	LONGHORNS	AMARILLO
CAPTAIN CHAPIN	HUSKIES	EL PASO
CARLISLE	INDIANS	PRICE
CARRIZO SPRINGS	WILDCATS	CARRIZO SPRINGS
CARROLL	DRAGONS	SOUTHLAKE
CARROLL, MARY	TIGERS	CORPUS CHRISTI

SCHOOL	MASCOT	CITY
CARROLLTON CHRISTIAN ACADEMY	SAINTS	CARROLLTON
CARTER, DAVID	COWBOYS	DALLAS
CARTER, JIMMY	COYOTES	LA JOYA
CARTER-RIVERSIDE	EAGLES	FORT WORTH
CARTHAGE	BULLDOGS	CARTHAGE
CASTLE HILLS FIRST BAPTIST	EAGLES	SAN ANTONIO
CASTLEBERRY	LIONS	RIVER OAKS
CATHEDRAL	IRISH	EL PASO
CATHEDRAL CHRISTIAN	WARRIORS	BEAUMONT
CAYUGA	WILDCATS	CAYUGA
CEDAR HILL	LONGHORNS	CEDAR HILL
CEDAR PARK	TIMBERWOLVES	CEDAR PARK
CELESTE	DEVILS, BLUE	CELESTE
CELINA	BOBCATS	CELINA
CENTENNIAL	TITANS	FRISCO
CENTER	ROUGHRIDERS	CENTER
CENTER POINT	PIRATES	CENTER POINT
CENTERVILLE	TIGERS	CENTERVILLE
CENTERVILLE	BULLDOGS	GROVETON
CENTRAL	CHARGERS	KELLER
CENTRAL	BULLDOGS	POLLOK
CENTRAL	JAGUARS	BEAUMONT
CENTRAL CATHOLIC	BUTTONS	SAN ANTONIO
CENTRAL HEIGHTS	DEVILS, BLUE	NACOGDOCHES
CENTRAL TEXAS CHRISTIAN	LIONS	TEMPLE
CHANNELVIEW	FALCONS	CHANNELVIEW
CHANNELVIEW CHRISTIAN	WARRIORS	CHANNELVIEW
CHANNING	EAGLES	CHANNING
CHAPEL HILL	BULLDOGS	TYLER
CHARLOTTE	TROJANS	CHARLOTTE
CHAVEZ	LOBOS	HOUSTON
CHEROKEE	INDIANS	CHEROKEE
CHESTER	YELLOWJACKETS	CHESTER
CHICO	DRAGONS	CHICO
CHILDRESS	BOBCATS	CHILDRESS
CHILLICOTHE	EAGLES	CHILLICOTHE
CHILTON	PIRATES	CHILTON

Port Aransas
Marlins

Fort Worth Bethesda
Ambassadors

Plano East
Panthers

San Saba
Armadillos

SCHOOL	MASCOT	CITY
CHINA SPRING	COUGARS	CHINA SPRING
CHINQUAPIN	BURRS	HIGHLAND
CHIRENO	OWLS	CHIRENO
CHISUM	MUSTANGS	PARIS
CHRIST COMMUNITY CHRISTIAN	MUSTANGS	AUSTIN
CHRIST THE KING	TROJANS	LUBBOCK
CHRISTIAN ACADEMY	EAGLES	ROWLETT
CHRISTIAN ACADEMY	KNIGHTS	JOSHUA
CHRISTIAN ACADEMY	MUSTANGS	McKINNEY
CHRISTIAN ACADEMY	WARRIORS	LUCAS
CHRISTIAN ACADEMY	WARRIORS	THE WOODLANDS
CHRISTIAN HERITAGE	CHARGERS	SAN ANTONIO
CHRISTIAN HERITAGE ACADEMY	EAGLES	BEAUMONT
CHRISTIAN LIFE CENTER	COUGARS	HUMBLE
CHRISTIAN LIFE FELLOWSHIP	WARRIORS	SEVEN POINTS
CHRISTOVAL	COUGARS	CHRISTOVAL
CHRISTWAY ACADEMY	CHAPARRALS	DUNCANVILLE
CHURCHILL	CHARGERS	SAN ANTONIO
CIGARROA	TOROS	LAREDO
CINCO RANCH	COUGARS	KATY
CISCO	LOBOES	CISCO
CISTERCIAN PREP	HAWKS	IRVING
CITY VIEW	MUSTANGS	WICHITA FALLS
CLARENDON	BRONCOS	CLARENDON
CLARK	COUGARS	PLANO
CLARK	COUGARS	SAN ANTONIO
CLARKSVILLE	TIGERS	CLARKSVILLE
CLASSICAL ACADEMY	KNIGHTS	MIDLAND
CLAUDE	MUSTANGS	CLAUDE
CLEAR BROOK	WOLVERINES	FRIENDSWOOD
CLEAR CREEK	WILDCATS	LEAGUE CITY
CLEAR LAKE	FALCONS	HOUSTON
CLEBURNE	YELLOWJACKETS	CLEBURNE
CLEMENS	BUFFALOES	SCHERTZ
CLEMENTS	RANGERS	SUGARLAND
CLEVELAND	INDIANS	CLEVELAND
CLIFTON	CUBS	CLIFTON
CLINT	LIONS	CLINT
CLYDE	BULLDOGS	CLYDE
COAHOMA	BULLDOGS	COAHOMA
COLDSPRING-OAKHURST	TROJANS	COLDSPRING
COLE	COUGARS	SAN ANTONIO
COLEMAN	BLUECATS	COLEMAN
COLLEYVILLE-HERITAGE	PANTHERS	COLLEYVILLE
COLLINS	TIGERS	KLEIN
COLLINSVILLE	PIRATES	COLLINSVILLE
COLMESNEIL	BULLDOGS	COLMESNEIL
COLORADO CITY	WOLVES	COLORADO CITY

SCHOOL	MASCOT	CITY
COLUMBIA	ROUGHNECKS	WEST COLUMBIA
COLUMBIA CHRISTIAN	WARRIORS	WEST COLUMBIA
COLUMBUS	CARDINALS	COLUMBUS
COMANCHE	INDIANS	COMANCHE
COMFORT	BOBCATS	COMFORT
COMMERCE	TIGERS	COMMERCE
COMMUNITY	BRAVES	NEVADA
COMMUNITY CHRISTIAN	LIONS	ORANGE
COMMUNITY CHRISTIAN	WARRIORS	CYPRESS
COMO PICTON	EAGLES	COMO
COMSTOCK	PANTHERS	COMSTOCK
CONCORDIA ACADEMY	CARDINALS	AUSTIN
CONCORDIA LUTHERAN	CRUSADERS	TOMBALL
CONNALLY	CADETS	WACO
CONNALLY	COUGARS	AUSTIN
CONROE	TIGERS	CONROE
COOLIDGE	YELLOWJACKETS	COOLIDGE
COOPER	COUGARS	ABILENE
COOPER	DRAGONS	THE WOODLANDS
COOPER	PIRATES	LUBBOCK
COOPER	BULLDOGS	COOPER
COPPELL	COWBOYS	COPPELL
COPPERAS COVE	BULLDOGS	COPPERAS COVE
CORNERSTONE CHRISTIAN	EAGLES	SAN ANTONIO
CORNERSTONE CHRISTIAN	EAGLES	WAXAHACHIE
CORONADO	MUSTANGS	LUBBOCK
CORONADO	THUNDERBIRDS	EL PASO
CORPUS CHRISTI ACADEMY	CAVALIERS	CORPUS CHRISTI
CORRIGAN CAMDEN	BULLDOGS	CORRIGAN
CORSICANA	TIGERS	CORSICANA
COTTON CENTER	ELKS	COTTON CENTER
COTULLA	COWBOYS	COTULLA
COUNTRY DAY	FALCONS	FORT WORTH
COVENANT CHRISTIAN	COUGARS	COLLEYVILLE
COVENANT CHRISTIAN	COUGARS	CONROE
COVENANT SCHOOL	KNIGHTS	DALLAS
COVINGTON	OWLS	COVINGTON
CRANDALL	PIRATES	CRANDALL
CRANE	CRANES, GOLDEN	CRANE
CRANFILLS GAP	LIONS	CRANFILLS GAP
CRAWFORD	PIRATES	CRAWFORD
CREEKVIEW	MUSTANGS	CARROLTON
CROCKETT	COUGARS	AUSTIN
CROCKETT	BULLDOGS	CROCKETT
CROSBY	COUGARS	CROSBY
CROSBYTON	CHIEFS	CROSBYTON
CROSS PLAINS	BUFFALOES	CROSS PLAINS
CROSSROADS	BOBCATS	MALAKOFF

152

SCHOOL	MASCOT	CITY
CROWELL	WILDCATS	CROWELL
CROWLEY	EAGLES	CROWLEY
CRYSTAL CITY	JAVELINAS	CRYSTAL CITY
CUERO	GOBBLERS	CUERO
CUMBY	TROJANS	CUMBY
CUSHING	BEARKATS	CUSHING
CY-FAIR (CYPRESS-FAIRBANKS)	BOBCATS	CYPRESS
CYPRESS CHRISTIAN	EAGLES	SPRING
CYPRESS CREEK	COUGARS	HOUSTON
CYPRESS FALLS	EAGLES	HOUSTON
CYPRESS RIDGE	RAMS	HOUSTON
CYPRESS SPRINGS	PANTHERS	CYPRESS
DAINGERFIELD	TIGERS	DAINGERFIELD
DALHART	WOLVES, GOLDEN	DALHART
DALLAS ACADEMY	EAGLES, GOLDEN	DALLAS
DALLAS CHRISTIAN	CHARGERS	MESQUITE
DANBURY	PANTHERS	DANBURY
DAVIS, JEFF	PANTHERS	HOUSTON
DAWSON	BULLDOGS	DAWSON
DAWSON	DRAGONS	WELCH
DAYTON	BRONCOS	DAYTON
DE LEON	BEARCATS	DE LEON
DE SOTO	EAGLES, FIGHTING	DE SOTO
DECATUR	EAGLES	DECATUR
DEER PARK	DEER	DEER PARK
DEKALB	BEARS	DEKALB
DEL RIO	RAMS	DEL RIO
DEL VALLE	CARDINALS	DEL VALLE
DEL VALLE	CONQUISTADORS	EL PASO
DELL CITY	COUGARS	DELL CITY
DENISON	YELLOWJACKETS	DENISON
DENTON	BRONCOS	DENTON
DENVER CITY	MUSTANGS	DENVER CITY
DESTINY	EAGLES, WILLING	SAN ANTONIO
DETROIT	EAGLES	DETROIT
DEVINE	WARHORSES	DEVINE
DEWEYVILLE	PIRATES	DEWEYVILLE
D'HANIS	COWBOYS	D'HANIS
DIAMOND HILL-JARVIS	EAGLES	FORT WORTH
DIBOLL	LUMBERJACKS	DIBOLL
DICKINSON	GATORS	DICKINSON
DILLEY	WOLVES	DILLEY
DIME BOX	LONGHORNS	DIME BOX
DIMMITT	BOBCATS	DIMMITT
DOBIE	LONGHORNS	HOUSTON
DODD CITY	HORNETS	DODD CITY
DONNA	REDSKINS	DONNA

153

SCHOOL	MASCOT	CITY
DOUGLASS	INDIANS	DOUGLASS
DRIPPING SPRINGS	TIGERS	DRIPPING SPRINGS
DUBLIN	LIONS	DUBLIN
DUCHESNE ACADEMY	CHARGERS	HOUSTON
DULLES	VIKINGS	SUGARLAND
DUMAS	DEMONS	DUMAS
DUNBAR	WILDCATS, FIGHTIN'	FORT WORTH
DUNCANVILLE	PANTHERS	DUNCANVILLE
EAGLE CHARTER	EAGLES	BEAUMONT
EAGLE PASS	EAGLES	EAGLE PASS
EARLY	LONGHORNS	EARLY
EAST BERNARD	BRAHMAS	EAST BERNARD
EAST CENTRAL	HORNETS	SAN ANTONIO
EAST CHAMBERS	BUCCANEERS	WINNIE
EAST TEXAS CHRISTIAN	PANTHERS	TYLER
EASTERN HILLS	HIGHLANDERS	FORT WORTH
EASTLAND	MAVERICKS	EASTLAND
EASTWOOD	TROOPERS	EL PASO
ECONOMEDES	JAGUARS	EDINBURG
ECTOR	EAGLES	ECTOR
EDCOUCH-ELSA	YELLOWJACKETS	EDCOUCH
EDEN	BULLDOGS	EDEN
EDGEWOOD	BULLDOGS	EDGEWOOD
EDINBURG	BOBCATS	EDINBURG
EDINBURG NORTH	COUGARS	EDINBURG
EDISON	BEARS, GOLDEN	SAN ANTONIO
EDNA	COWBOYS	EDNA
EISENHOWER	EAGLES	HOUSTON
EL CAMPO	RICEBIRDS	EL CAMPO
EL DORADO	AZTECS	EL PASO
EL PASO HIGH	TIGERS	EL PASO
EL PASO SCHOOL OF EXCELLENCE	DOLPHINS	EL PASO
ELDORADO	EAGLES	ELDORADO
ELECTRA	TIGERS	ELECTRA
ELGIN	WILDCATS	ELGIN
ELKHART	ELKS	ELKHART
ELKINS	KNIGHTS	MISSOURI CITY
ELLISON	EAGLES	KILLEEN
ELSIK	RAMS	ALIEF
ELYSIAN FIELDS	YELLOWJACKETS	ELYSIAN FIELDS
EMERY	JAGUARS	HOUSTON
EMMANUEL BAPTIST	LIONS	IRVING
EMPOWERMENT ACADEMY	PANTHERS	AUSTIN
ENCOURAGER CHRISTIAN	WARRIORS, MIGHTY	HOUSTON
ENNIS	LIONS	ENNIS
EPISCOPAL	KNIGHTS	BELLAIRE
EPISCOPAL SCHOOL OF DALLAS	EAGLES	DALLAS

SCHOOL	MASCOT	CITY
ERA	HORNETS	ERA
ESTACADO	MATADORS	LUBBOCK
EULA	PIRATES	CLYDE
EUSTACE	BULLDOGS	EUSTACE
EVADALE	REBELS	EVADALE
EVANGEL TEMPLE CHRISTIAN	EAGLES	GRAND PRAIRIE
EVANT	ELKS	EVANT
EVERMAN	BULLDOGS	EVERMAN
FABENS	WILDCATS	FABENS
FAIRFIELD	EAGLES	FAIRFIELD
FAIRHILL SCHOOL	FALCONS	DALLAS
FAITH	COUGARS	VICTORIA
FAITH ACADEMY	KNIGHTS	BELLVILLE
FAITH CHRISTIAN	LIONS	EL PASO
FAITH CHRISTIAN	LIONS	GRAPEVINE
FAITH CHRISTIAN	SAINTS	PASADENA
FAITH FAMILY ACADEMY	EAGLES	DALLAS
FAITH WEST ACADEMY	EAGLES	KATY
FALFURRIAS	JERSEYS	FALFURRIAS
FALLS CITY	BEAVERS	FALLS CITY
FAMILY CHRISTIAN	WARRIORS	HOUSTON
FANNINDEL	FALCONS	LADONIA
FARMERSVILLE	FARMERS, FIGHTING	FARMERSVILLE
FARMERSVILLE CHRISTIAN ACADEMY	WARRIORS	FARMERSVILLE
FARWELL	STEERS	FARWELL
FAYETTEVILLE	LIONS	FAYETTEVILLE
FELLOWSHIP ACADEMY	MUSTANGS	ARLINGTON
FERRIS	YELLOWJACKETS	FERRIS
FIRST BAPTIST	WARRIORS	PASADENA
FIRST BAPTIST ACADEMY	EAGLES	UNIVERSAL CITY
FIRST BAPTIST ACADEMY	SAINTS	DALLAS
FLATONIA	BULLDOGS	FLATONIA
FLORENCE	BUFFALOES	FLORENCE
FLORESVILLE	TIGERS	FLORESVILLE
FLOUR BLUFF	HORNETS	CORPUS CHRISTI
FLOWER MOUND	JAGUARS	FLOWER MOUND

Quinlan Ford
Panthers

Baytown Robert E. Lee
Ganders

Brownfield
Cubs

Arlington
Colts

SCHOOL	MASCOT	CITY
FLOYDADA	WHIRLWINDS	FLOYDADA
FOLLETT	PANTHERS	FOLLETT
FORD WH	PANTHERS	QUINLAN
FOREST BROOK	JAGUARS	HOUSTON
FORESTBURG	LONGHORNS	FORESTBURG
FORNEY	JACKRABBITS	FORNEY
FORSAN	BUFFALOES	FORSAN
FORT BEND BAPTIST	EAGLES	SUGARLAND
FORT BEND BAPTIST ACADEMY	EAGLES	SUGARLAND
FORT DAVIS	INDIANS	FORT DAVIS
FORT ELLIOT	COUGARS	BRISCOE
FORT HANCOCK	MUSTANGS	FORT HANCOCK
FORT STOCKTON	PANTHERS	FORT STOCKTON
FORT WORTH CHRISTIAN	CARDINALS	FORT WORTH
FOSSIL RIDGE	PANTHERS	KELLER
FOSTER	FALCONS	RICHMOND
FOX TECH	BUFFALOES	SAN ANTONIO
FRANKLIN	COUGARS	EL PASO
FRANKLIN	LIONS	FRANKLIN
FRANKSTON	INDIANS	FRANKSTON
FREDERICKSBURG	BILLIES, BATTLIN'	FREDERICKSBURG
FREER	BUCKAROOS	FREER
FRENSHIP	TIGERS	WOLFFORTH
FRIENDSWOOD	MUSTANGS	FRIENDSWOOD
FRIONA	CHIEFTAINS	FRIONA
FRISCO	RACCOONS	FRISCO
FROST	POLAR BEARS	FROST
FRUITVALE	BOBCATS	FRUITVALE
FULTON ACADEMY	FALCONS	HEATH
FURR	BRAHMA BULLS	HOUSTON
GAINESVILLE	LEOPARDS	GAINESVILLE
GAINESVILLE STATE	TORNADOS	GAINESVILLE
GALENA PARK	YELLOWJACKETS	GALENA PARK
GANADO	INDIANS	GANADO
GARDEN CITY	BEARKATS	GARDEN CITY
GARLAND	OWLS	GARLAND
GARLAND CHRISTIAN ACADEMY	SWORDSMEN	GARLAND
GARRISON	BULLDOGS	GARRISON
GARY	BOBCATS	GARY
GATESVILLE	HORNETS, FIGHTING	GATESVILLE
GATEWAY	EAGLES	SAN ANTONIO
GATEWAY SCHOOL	GATORS	ARLINGTON
GEORGE WEST	LONGHORNS	GEORGE WEST
GEORGETOWN	EAGLES	GEORGETOWN
GERVIN	COYOTES	SAN ANTONIO
GIDDINGS	BUFFALOES	GIDDINGS
GIDDINGS STATE	INDIANS	GIDDINGS

SCHOOL	MASCOT	CITY
GILMER	BUCKEYES	GILMER
GLADEWATER	BEARS	GLADEWATER
GLEN ROSE	TIGERS	GLEN ROSE
GLENVIEW CHRISTIAN	COWBOYS	FORT WORTH
GODLEY	WILDCATS	GODLEY
GOLD-BERG	BEARS	BOWIE
GOLDTHWAITE	EAGLES	GOLDTHWAITE
GOLIAD	TIGERS	GOLIAD
GONZALES	APACHES	GONZALES
GOODRICH	HORNETS	GOODRICH
GORDON	LONGHORNS	GORDON
GORMAN	PANTHERS	GORMAN
GOSPEL LIGHTHOUSE CHRISTIAN	LEOPARDS	DALLAS
GOVERNMENT & LAW, MAGNET SCHOOL FOR	EAGLES	DALLAS
GRACE CHRISTIAN ACADEMY	EAGLES	HOUSTON
GRACE COMMUNITY	COUGARS	TYLER
GRACE PREP ACADEMY	LIONS	ARLINGTON
GRADY	WILDCATS	LENORAH
GRAFORD	JACKRABBITS	GRAFORD
GRAHAM	STEERS	GRAHAM
GRANBURY	PIRATES	GRANBURY
GRAND PRAIRIE	GOPHERS	GRAND PRAIRIE
GRAND SALINE	INDIANS	GRAND SALINE
GRANDFALLS-ROYALTY	COWBOYS	GRANDFALLS
GRANDVIEW	ZEBRAS	GRANDVIEW
GRANGER	LIONS	GRANGER
GRAPE CREEK	EAGLES	SAN ANGELO
GRAPELAND	SANDIES	GRAPELAND
GRAPEVINE	MUSTANGS	GRAPEVINE
GREAT HILLS CHRISTIAN	EAGLES	AUSTIN
GREENHILL	HORNETS	ADDISON
GREENVILLE	LIONS	GREENVILLE
GREENVILLE CHRISTIAN	EAGLES	GREENVILLE
GREENWOOD	RANGERS	MIDLAND
GREGORY-PORTLAND	WILDCATS	PORTLAND
GROESBECK	GOATS	GROESBECK
GROOM	TIGERS	GROOM
GROVETON	INDIANS	GROVETON
GRUVER	GREYHOUNDS	GRUVER
GUNTER	TIGERS	GUNTER
GUSTINE	TIGERS	GUSTINE
GUTHRIE	JAGUARS	GUTHRIE
GUYER	WILDCATS	DENTON
HALE CENTER	OWLS	HALE CENTER
HALLETTSVILLE	BRAHMAS	HALLETTSVILLE
HALLSVILLE	BOBCATS	HALLSVILLE
HALTOM	BUFFALOES	HALTOM

SCHOOL	MASCOT	CITY
HAMILTON	BULLDOGS	HAMILTON
HAMLIN	PIED PIPERS	HAMLIN
HAMSHIRE-FANNETT	LONGHORNS	HAMSHIRE
HANKS	KNIGHTS	EL PASO
HANNA	EAGLES	BROWNSVILLE
HAPPY	COWBOYS	HAPPY
HAPPY HILL	PIONEERS	GRANBURY
HARDIN	HORNETS	HARDIN
HARDIN-JEFFERSON	HAWKS	SOUR LAKE
HARGRAVE	FALCONS	HUFFMAN
HARKER HEIGHTS	KNIGHTS	HARKER HEIGHTS
HARLANDALE	INDIANS	SAN ANTONIO
HARLETON	WILDCATS	HARLETON
HARLINGEN	CARDINALS	HARLINGEN
HARLINGEN SOUTH	HAWKS	HARLINGEN
HARMONY	EAGLES	HARMONY
HARPER	LONGHORNS	HARPER
HARROLD	HORNETS	HARROLD
HART	LONGHORNS	HART
HARTLEY	TIGERS	HARTLEY
HARVEST CHRISTIAN	OWLS	FORT WORTH
HARVEST CHRISTIAN	SAINTS	PASADENA
HARVEST CHRISTIAN	SAINTS	WATAUGA
HARVEST SCHOOL	FALCONS	SAN ANTONIO
HASKELL	INDIANS	HASKELL
HASTINGS	BEARS, FIGHTING	ALIEF
HAWKINS	HAWKS	HAWKINS
HAWLEY	BEARCATS	HAWLEY
HAYS	REBELS	BUDA
HEALEY-MURPHY	TROJANS	SAN ANTONIO
HEALTH CAREERS	PHOENIX	SAN ANTONIO
HEALTH PROFESSIONS, MAGNET SCHOOL FOR	LIONS	DALLAS
HEARNE	EAGLES	HEARNE
HEATH	HAWKS	ROCKWALL
HEBBRONVILLE	LONGHORNS	HEBBRONVILLE
HEBRON	HAWKS	CARROLTON
HEDLEY	OWLS	HEDLEY

Friendswood
Clear Brook
Wolverines

Winters
Blizzards

Grand Prairie
Gophers

Albany
Lions

158

SCHOOL	MASCOT	CITY
HEMPHILL	HORNETS	HEMPHILL
HEMPSTEAD	BOBCATS	HEMPSTEAD
HENDERSON	LIONS	HENDERSON
HENDRICKSON	HAWKS	PFLUGERVILLE
HENRIETTA	BEARCATS	HENRIETTA
HEREFORD	WHITEFACES	HEREFORD
HERITAGE	EAGLES	FREDERICKSBURG
HERITAGE CHRISTIAN	EAGLES	HUNTSVILLE
HERITAGE CHRISTIAN ACADEMY	EAGLES	ROCKWALL
HERMLEIGH	CARDINALS	HERMLEIGH
HICO	TIGERS	HICO
HIDALGO	PIRATES	HIDALGO
HIGGINS	COYOTES	HIGGINS
HIGH ISLAND	CARDINALS	HIGH ISLAND
HIGHLAND	HORNETS	ROSCOE
HIGHLAND AVENUE	WARRIORS	ARANSAS PASS
HIGHLAND PARK	HORNETS	AMARILLO
HIGHLAND PARK	SCOTS	DALLAS
HIGHLANDS	OWLS	SAN ANTONIO
HIGHLANDS	TRAIL BLAZERS	IRVING
HIGHTOWER	HURRICANES	MISSOURI CITY
HILL COUNTRY CHRISTIAN	KNIGHTS	KERRVILLE
HILL SCHOOL	HAWKS	FORT WORTH
HILLCREST	PANTHERS	DALLAS
HILLSBORO	EAGLES	HILLSBORO
HIRSCHI	HUSKIES	WICHITA FALLS
HITCHCOCK	BULLDOGS	HITCHCOCK
HOCKADAY	DAISIES	DALLAS
HOLLAND	HORNETS	HOLLAND
HOLLIDAY	EAGLES, FIGHTING	HOLLIDAY
HOLMES	HUSKIES	SAN ANTONIO
HOLY CROSS	KNIGHTS	SAN ANTONIO
HOLY CROSS ACADEMY	MUSTANGS	AMARILLO
HOLY TRINITY CATHOLIC	CELTICS	TEMPLE
HONDO	OWLS	HONDO
HONEY GROVE	WARRIORS	HONEY GROVE
HONORS UNIVERSITY HIGH	BULLDOGS	DALLAS
HOOKS	HORNETS	HOOKS
HORIZON	SCORPIONS	CLINT
HORN	JAGUARS	MESQUITE
HOUSTON	HURRICANES	SAN ANTONIO
HOUSTON	TEXANS	ARLINGTON
HOUSTON	TIGERS	HOUSTON
HOUSTON CHRISTIAN	MUSTANGS	HOUSTON
HOWE	BULLDOGS	HOWE
HUBBARD	JAGUARS	HUBBARD
HUCKABAY	INDIANS	STEPHENVILLE
HUDSON	HORNETS	LUFKIN

SCHOOL	MASCOT	CITY
HUGHES SPRINGS	MUSTANGS	HUGHES SPRINGS
HULL-DAISETTA	BOBCATS	DAISETTA
HUMBLE	WILDCATS	HUMBLE
HUNTINGTON	DEVILS, RED	HUNTINGTON
HUNTSVILLE	HORNETS	HUNTSVILLE
HUTCHINS	EAGLES	DALLAS
HUTTO	HIPPOS	HUTTO
HYDE PARK CENTRAL BAPTIST	PANTHERS	AUSTIN
IDALOU	WILDCATS	IDALOU
IDEA ACADEMY	TITANS	DONNA
INCARNATE WORD	SHAMROCKS, LADY	SAN ANTONIO
INCARNATE WORD ACADEMY	FALCONS	HOUSTON
INCARNATE WORD ACADEMY	ANGELS	CORPUS
INDUSTRIAL	COBRAS	VANDERBILT
INGLESIDE	MUSTANGS	INGLESIDE
INTERNATIONAL NEWCOMERS ACADEMY	DRAGONS	FORT WORTH
IOLA	BULLDOGS	IOLA
IOWA PARK	HAWKS	IOWA PARK
IRA	BULLDOGS	IRA
IRAAN	BRAVES	IRAAN
IREDELL	DRAGONS	IREDELL
IRION COUNTY	HORNETS	MERTZON
IRVIN	ROCKETS	EL PASO
IRVING	TIGERS	IRVING
ITALY	GLADIATORS	ITALY
ITASCA	WAMPUS CATS	ITASCA
JACKSBORO	TIGERS	JACKSBORO
JACKSONVILLE	INDIANS, FIGHTING	JACKSONVILLE
JARRELL	COUGARS	JARRELL
JASPER	BULLDOGS	JASPER
JASPER	JAGUARS	PLANO
JAY, JOHN	MUSTANGS	SAN ANTONIO
JAYTON	JAYBIRDS	JAYTON
JEFFERSON	BULLDOGS	JEFFERSON
JEFFERSON	FOXES, SILVER	EL PASO
JEFFERSON	MUSTANGS	SAN ANTONIO
JEFFERSON	PATRIOTS	DALLAS
JERSEY VILLAGE	FALCONS	HOUSTON
JESSE JACKSON ACADEMY	JAGUARS	HOUSTON
JESUIT COLLEGE PREP	RANGERS	DALLAS
JESUS CHAPEL	CHARGERS	EL PASO
JIM NED	INDIANS	TUSCOLA
JOAQUIN	RAMS	JOAQUIN
JOHN PAUL II	CARDINALS	PLANO
JOHNSON, LB	EAGLES	JOHNSON CITY
JOHNSON, LB	JAGUARS	AUSTIN

SCHOOL	MASCOT	CITY
JOHNSON, LB	WOLVES	LAREDO
JOHNSTON	RAMS	AUSTIN
JONES, A C	TROJANS	BEEVILLE
JONES, JESSE	FALCONS	HOUSTON
JONESBORO	EAGLES	JONESBORO
JORDAN, BARBARA	JAGUARS	HOUSTON
JOSHUA	OWLS, FIGHTING	JOSHUA
JOURDANTON	INDIANS	JOURDANTON
JUÁREZ-LINCOLN	COYOTES	LA JOYA
JUDSON	ROCKETS	CONVERSE
JUNCTION	EAGLES	JUNCTION
KARNACK	INDIANS	KARNACK
KARNES CITY	BADGERS	KARNES CITY
KASHMERE	RAMS, FIGHTING	HOUSTON
KATY	TIGERS	KATY
KAUFMAN	LIONS	KAUFMAN
KEENE	CHARGERS	KEENE
KELLER	INDIANS	KELLER
KELTON	LIONS	KELTON?
KEMP	YELLOWJACKETS	KEMP
KEMPNER	COUGARS	SUGARLAND
KENEDY	LIONS	KENEDY
KENNARD	TIGERS	KENNARD
KENNEDALE	PANTHERS	KENNEDALE
KENNEDY, JF	ROCKETS	SAN ANTONIO
KERENS	BOBCATS	KERENS
KERMIT	YELLOWJACKETS	KERMIT
KERR	TIGERS	ALIEF
KEYS HIGH SCHOOL	PHOENIX	EULESS
KEYSTONE	COBRAS	SAN ANTONIO
KILGORE	BULLDOGS	KILGORE
KILLEEN	KANGAROOS	KILLEEN
KIMBALL	KNIGHTS	DALLAS
KING	MUSTANGS	CORPUS CHRISTI
KING	PANTHERS	HOUSTON
KING	BRAHMAS	KINGSVILLE
KINGSVILLE ACADEMY	LIONS, PRIDE OF	KINGSVILLE
KINGWOOD	MUSTANGS	KINGWOOD
KINKAID	FALCONS	HOUSTON
KIRBYVILLE	WILDCATS	KIRBYVILLE
KLEIN	BEARKATS	KLEIN
KLEIN FOREST	EAGLES, GOLDEN	HOUSTON
KLEIN OAK	PANTHERS	SPRING
KLONDIKE	COUGARS	KLONDIKE
KNIPPA	ROCKCRUSHERS	KNIPPA
KNOX CITY	GREYHOUNDS	KNOX CITY
KOPPERL	EAGLES	KOPPERL

SCHOOL	MASCOT	CITY
KOUNTZE	LIONS	KOUNTZE
KRESS	KANGAROOS	KRESS
KRUM	BOBCATS	KRUM
LA FERIA	LIONS	LA FERIA
LA GRANGE	LEOPARDS	LA GRANGE
LA JOYA	COYOTES	LA JOYA
LA MARQUE	COUGARS	LA MARQUE
LA PORTE	BULLDOGS	LA PORTE
LA POYNOR	FLYERS	LA RUE
LA PRYOR	BULLDOGS	LA PRYOR
LA VEGA	PIRATES	WACO
LA VERNIA	BEARS	LA VERNIA
LA VILLA	CARDINALS, FIGHTING	LA VILLA
LAGO VISTA	VIKINGS	LAGO VISTA
LAKE COUNTRY CHRISTIAN	EAGLES	FORT WORTH
LAKE DALLAS	FALCONS	CORINTH
LAKE HIGHLANDS	WILDCATS	DALLAS
LAKE TRAVIS	CAVALIERS	AUSTIN
LAKE VIEW	CHIEFS	SAN ANGELO
LAKE WORTH	BULLFROGS	FORT WORTH
LAKEHILL PREP	WARRIORS	DALLAS
LAKEVIEW	EAGLES	LAKEVIEW
LAKEVIEW CENTENNIAL	PATRIOTS	GARLAND
LAKEWOOD PRESBYTERIAN	KNIGHTS	DALLAS
LAMAR	MUSTANGS	ROSENBERG
LAMAR	REDSKINS	HOUSTON
LAMAR	VIKINGS	ARLINGTON
LAMESA	TORNADOES, GOLDEN	LAMESA
LAMPASAS	BADGERS	LAMPASAS
LANCASTER	TIGERS	LANCASTER
LANDMARK BAPTIST	BLAZERS	MEXIA
LANEVILLE	YELLOWJACKETS	LANEVILLE
LANGHAM CREEK	LOBOS	HOUSTON
LANIER	VIKINGS	AUSTIN
LANIER	VOKS	SAN ANTONIO
LATEXO	TIGERS	LATEXO
LAZBUDDIE	LONGHORNS	LAZBUDDIE
LEAKEY	EAGLES	LEAKEY
LEANDER	LIONS	LEANDER
LEE	GANDERS	BAYTOWN
LEE	GENERALS	HOUSTON
LEE	RAIDERS, RED	TYLER
LEE	REBELS	MIDLAND
LEE	VOLUNTEERS	SAN ANTONIO
LEFORS	PIRATES	LEFORS
LEGACY CHRISTIAN ACADEMY	EAGLES	FRISCO
LEGACY OAKS CHRISTIAN	LIONS	AUSTIN

SCHOOL	MASCOT	CITY
LEGGETT	PIRATES	LEGGETT
LEON	COUGARS	JEWETT
LEONARD	TIGERS	LEONARD
LEVELLAND	LOBOS	LEVELLAND
LEVERETT'S CHAPEL	LIONS	LEVERETT'S CHAPEL
LEWISVILLE	FARMERS	LEWISVILLE
LEXINGTON	EAGLES	LEXINGTON
LIBERTY	PANTHERS	LIBERTY
LIBERTY CHRISTIAN	WARRIORS	LIBERTY
LIBERTY EYLAU	LEOPARDS	TEXARKANA
LIBERTY HILL	PANTHERS	LIBERTY HILL
LIFE CHRISTIAN ACADEMY	EAGLES	HOUSTON
LIFEGATE CHRISTIAN	FALCONS	SEGUIN
LIFESTYLE CHRISTIAN	VICTORS	CONROE
LINCOLN	TIGERS	DALLAS
LINDALE	EAGLES	LINDALE
LINDEN-KILDARE	TIGERS	LINDEN
LINDSAY	KNIGHTS	LINDSAY
LINGLEVILLE	CARDINALS	LINGLEVILLE
LIPAN	INDIANS	LIPAN
LITTLE CYPRESS-MAURICEVILLE	BEARS	ORANGE
LITTLE ELM	LOBOS	LITTLE ELM
LITTLEFIELD	WILDCATS	LITTLEFIELD
LIVING FAITH	EAGLES	DICKENSON
LIVING STONES CHRISTIAN	LIONS	ALVIN
LIVING WATERS CHRISTIAN	CHALLENGERS	ROSENBERG
LIVING WORD ACADEMY	EAGLES	IRVING
LIVINGSTON	LIONS	LIVINGSTON
LIVINGWAY CHRISTIAN	WARRIORS	BROWNSVILLE
LLANO	YELLOWJACKETS	LLANO
LOCKHART	LIONS	LOCKHART
LOCKNEY	LONGHORNS	LOCKNEY
LOHN	EAGLES	LOHN
LOMETA	HORNETS	LOMETA
LONE OAK	BUFFALOES	LONE OAK
LONGVIEW	LOBOS	LONGVIEW
LOOP	LONGHORNS	LOOP

Laredo Martin
Tigers

El Paso
Del Valle
Conquistadors

Watauga
Harvest Christian
Academy Saints

Breckenridge
Buckaroos

SCHOOL	MASCOT	CITY
LOPEZ	LOBOS	BROWNSVILLE
LORAINE	BULLDOGS	LORAINE
LORENA	LEOPARDS	LORENA
LORENZO	HORNETS	LORENZO
LORETTO ACADEMY	ANGELS	EL PASO
LOS FRESNOS	FALCONS	LOS FRESNOS
LOUISE	HORNETS	LOUISE
LOVELADY	LIONS	LOVELADY
LUBBOCK	WESTERNERS	LUBBOCK
LUBBOCK CHRISTIAN	EAGLES	LUBBOCK
LUEDERS-AVOCA	RAIDERS	AVOCA
LUFKIN	PANTHERS	LUFKIN
LULING	EAGLES	LULING
LUMBERTON	RAIDERS	LUMBERTON
LUTHERAN	LIONS	DALLAS
LUTHERAN	MUSTANGS	SAN ANTONIO
LUTHERAN NORTH	LIONS	HOUSTON
LUTHERAN SOUTH	PIONEERS	HOUSTON
LYDIA PATTERSON	LIONS	EL PASO
LYFORD	BULLDOGS	LYFORD
LYTLE	PIRATES	LYTLE
MABANK	PANTHERS	MABANK
MAC ARTHUR	BRAHMAS	SAN ANTONIO
MAC ARTHUR	CARDINALS	IRVING
MAC ARTHUR	GENERALS	HOUSTON
MADISON	MARLINS	HOUSTON
MADISON	MAVERICKS	SAN ANTONIO
MADISON	TROJANS	DALLAS
MADISONVILLE	MUSTANGS	MADISONVILLE
MAGNOLIA	BULLDOGS	MAGNOLIA
MALAKOFF	TIGERS	MALAKOFF
MANOR	MUSTANGS	MANOR
MANSFIELD	JAGUARS	MANSFIELD
MARATHON	MUSTANGS	MARATHON
MARBLE FALLS	MUSTANGS	MARBLE FALLS
MARCUS	MARAUDERS	FLOWER MOUND
MARFA	SHORTHORNS	MARFA
MARINE MILITARY ACADEMY	LEATHERNECKS	HARLINGEN
MARION	BULLDOGS	MARION
MARLIN	BULLDOGS	MARLIN
MARSHALL, JOHN	MAVERICKS	MARSHALL
MARSHALL, JOHN	RAMS	SAN ANTONIO
MARSHALL, THURGOOD	BULLDOGS	MISSOURI CITY
MART	PANTHERS	MART
MARTIN	TIGERS	LAREDO
MARTIN	WARRIORS	ARLINGTON
MARTIN'S MILL	MUSTANGS	BEN WHEELER

164

SCHOOL	MASCOT	CITY
MARTINSVILLE	PIRATES	MARTINSVILLE
MASON	PUNCHERS	MASON
MASONIC HOME	MIGHTY MITES	FT WORTH
MATHIS	PIRATES	MATHIS
MAUD	CARDINALS	MAUD
MAY	TIGERS	MAY
MAYDE CREEK	RAMS	HOUSTON
MAYPEARL	PANTHERS	MAYPEARL
McALLEN	BULLDOGS	McALLEN
McCALLUM	KNIGHTS	AUSTIN
McCAMEY	BADGERS	McCAMEY
McCOLLUM	COWBOYS	SAN ANTONIO
McGREGOR	BULLDOGS	McGREGOR
McKINNEY	LIONS	McKINNEY
McLEAN	TIGERS	McLEAN
McLEOD	LONGHORNS	McLEOD
McMULLEN COUNTY	COWBOYS	TILDEN
McNEIL	MAVERICKS	AUSTIN
MEADOW	BRONCOS	MEADOW
MEDINA	BOBCATS	MEDINA
MEDINA VALLEY	PANTHERS	CASTROVILLE
MEGARGEL	MUSTANGS	MEGARGEL
MELISSA	CARDINALS	MELISSA
MEMORIAL	MAVERICKS	PASADENA
MEMORIAL	VIPERS	VICTORIA
MEMORIAL	MINUTEMEN	SAN ANTONIO
MEMORIAL	MUSTANGS	HOUSTON
MEMORIAL	MUSTANGS	McALLEN
MEMORIAL	TITANS	PORT ARTHUR
MEMORIAL	WOLVERINES	ALAMO
MEMORIAL HALL	COUGARS	HOUSTON
MEMPHIS	CYCLONES	MEMPHIS
MENARD	YELLOWJACKETS	MENARD
MERCEDES	TIGERS	MERCEDES
MERCEDES ACADEMY	TIGERS, WHITE BENGAL	MERCEDES
MERIDIAN	YELLOWJACKETS	MERIDIAN
MERKEL	BADGERS	MERKEL
MESQUITE	SKEETERS	MESQUITE
METHODIST HOME BOYS RANCH	MUSTANGS	WACO
METRO OPPORTUNITY SCHOOL	FALCONS	FORT WORTH
METROPOLITAN CHRISTIAN	EAGLES	DALLAS
MEXIA	BLACKCATS	MEXIA
MIAMI	WARRIORS	MIAMI
MIDLAND	BULLDOGS	MIDLAND
MIDLAND CHRISTIAN	MUSTANGS	MIDLAND
MIDLOTHIAN	PANTHERS	MIDLOTHIAN
MIDWAY	FALCONS	HENRIETTA
MIDWAY	PANTHERS	HEWITT

SCHOOL	MASCOT	CITY
MILANO	EAGLES	MILANO
MILBY	BUFFALOES	HOUSTON
MILDRED	EAGLES	MILDRED
MILES	BULLDOGS	MILES
MILFORD	BULLDOGS	MILFORD
MILLER	BUCCANEERS	CORPUS
MILLER GROVE	HORNETS	CUMBY
MILLSAP	BULLDOGS	MILLSAP
MINEOLA	YELLOWJACKETS	MINEOLA
MINERAL WELLS	RAMS	MINERAL WELLS
MISSION	EAGLES	MISSION
MOLINA	JAGUARS	DALLAS
MONAHANS	LOBOS	MONAHANS
MONTEREY	PLAINSMEN	LUBBOCK
MONTGOMERY	BEARS	MONTGOMERY
MONTWOOD	RAMS	EL PASO
MOODY	TROJANS	CORPUS CHRISTI
MOODY	BEARCATS	MOODY
MOORE,TOM	WARRIORS	INGRAM
MORAN	BULLDOGS	MORAN
MORGAN	EAGLES	MORGAN
MORRIS ACADEMY	PRAYING HANDS	HOUSTON
MORTON	INDIANS	MORTON
MORTON RANCH	MAVERICKS	KATY
MOTLEY COUNTY	MATADORS	MATADOR
MOULTON	BOBKATZ	MOULTON
MOUNT CARMEL	REBELS	HOUSTON
MOUNT ENTERPRISE	WILDCATS	MOUNT ENTERPRISE
MOUNT PLEASANT	TIGERS	MOUNT PLEASANT
MOUNT VERNON	TIGERS	MOUNT VERNON
MOUNTAIN VIEW	LOBOS	EL PASO
MSGR. KELLY	BULLDOGS	BEAUMONT
MUENSTER	HORNETS	MUENSTER
MULESHOE	MULES	MULESHOE
MULLIN	BULLDOGS	MULLIN
MUMFORD	MUSTANGS	MUMFORD
MUNDAY	MOGULS	MUNDAY

Devine
Warhorses

South Garland
Colonels

Arlington Lamar
Vikings

Clyde
Bulldogs

SCHOOL	MASCOT	CITY
NAAMAN FOREST	RANGERS	GARLAND
NAGOGDOCHES	DRAGONS	NAGOGDOCHES
NATALIA	MUSTANGS	NATALIA
NAVARRO	PANTHERS	GERONIMO
NAVASOTA	RATTLERS	NAVASOTA
NAZARETH	SWIFTS	NAZARETH
NECHES	TIGERS	NECHES
NEDERLAND	BULLDOGS	NEDERLAND
NEEDVILLE	BLUEJAYS	NEEDVILLE
NEW BOSTON	LIONS	NEW BOSTON
NEW BRAUNFELS	UNICORNS	NEW BRAUNFELS
NEW BRAUNFELS CHRISTIAN	BOBCATS	NEW BRAUNFELS
NEW CANEY	EAGLES	NEW CANEY
NEW DEAL	LIONS	NEW DEAL
NEW DIANA	EAGLES	DIANA
NEW HOME	LEOPARDS	NEW HOME
NEW LIFE CHRISTIAN ACADEMY	EAGLES	SAN ANTONIO
NEW SUMMERFIELD	HORNETS	NEW SUMMERFIELD
NEW WAVERLY	BULLDOGS	NEW WAVERLY
NEWCASTLE	BOBCATS	NEWCASTLE
NEWTON	EAGLES	NEWTON
NEY	WIZARDS	NEW BRAUNFELS
NIMITZ	COUGARS	HOUSTON
NIMITZ	VIKINGS	IRVING
NIXON, JW	MUSTANGS	LAREDO
NIXON-SMILEY	MUSTANGS	NIXON
NOCONA	INDIANS	NOCONA
NOLAN CATHOLIC	VIKINGS	FORT WORTH
NORDHEIM	PIRATES	NORDHEIM
NORMANGEE	PANTHERS	NORMANGEE
NORTH	BULLDOGS	McKINNEY
NORTH CROWLEY	PANTHERS	FORT WORTH
NORTH DALLAS	BULLDOGS	DALLAS
NORTH GARLAND	RAIDERS	GARLAND
NORTH HOPKINS	PANTHERS	SULPHUR SPRINGS
NORTH HOUSTON BAPTIST	EAGLES	HOUSTON
NORTH LAMAR	PANTHERS	PARIS
NORTH MESQUITE	STALLIONS	MESQUITE
NORTH SHORE	MUSTANGS	HOUSTON
NORTH SIDE	STEERS	VERNON
NORTH ZULCH	BULLDOGS	NORTH ZULCH
NORTHBROOK	RAIDERS	HOUSTON
NORTHEAST CHRISTIAN ACADEMY	WARRIORS	KINGWOOD
NORTHLAND CHRISTIAN	COUGARS	HOUSTON
NORTHSIDE	INDIANS	VERNON
NORTHWEST	TEXANS	JUSTIN
NORTHWEST ACADEMY	CRUSADERS	HOUSTON
NOTRE DAME	KNIGHTS	WICHITA FALLS

SCHOOL	MASCOT	CITY
NOVICE	HORNETS	NOVICE
NUECES CANYON	PANTHERS	BARKSDALE
OAK RIDGE	EAGLES, WAR	CONROE
OAK TRAIL CHRISTIAN ACADEMY	EAGLES	GRANBURY
OAKRIDGE	OWLS	ARLINGTON
OAKWOOD	PANTHERS	OAKWOOD
O'CONNELL	BUCCANEERS	GALVESTON
O'CONNOR, SANDRA	PANTHERS	HELOTES
ODEM	OWLS	ODEM
ODESSA	BRONCOS	ODESSA
O'DONNELL	EAGLES	O'DONNELL
OGLESBY	TIGERS	OGLESBY
OLNEY	CUBS	OLNEY
OLTON	MUSTANGS	OLTON
ONALASKA	WILDCATS	ONALASKA
ORANGE GROVE	BULLDOGS	ORANGE GROVE
ORANGEFIELD	BOBCATS	ORANGEFIELD
ORE CITY	REBELS	ORE CITY
OUR LADY OF GRACE	LIONS	DALLAS
OUR LADY OF THE HILLS	HAWKS	KERRVILLE
OVERTON	MUSTANGS	OVERTON
OVILLA	EAGLES	RED OAK
OZEN	PANTHERS	BEAUMONT
OZONA	LIONS	OZONA
PACE	VIKINGS	BROWNSVILLE
PADUCAH	DRAGONS	PADUCAH
PAINT CREEK	PIRATES	HASKELL
PAINT ROCK	INDIANS	PAINT ROCK
PALACIOS	SHARKS	PALACIOS
PALESTINE	WILDCATS	PALESTINE
PALMER	BULLDOGS	PALMER
PALO DURO	DONS	AMARILLO
PAMPA	HARVESTERS	PAMPA
PANHANDLE	PANTHERS	PANHANDLE
PANTEGO CHRISTIAN	PANTHERS	ARLINGTON
PANTHER CREEK	PANTHERS	VALERA
PARADISE	PANTHERS	PARADISE
PARIS	WILDCATS	PARIS
PARKLAND	MATADORS	EL PASO
PARKVIEW CHRISTIAN ACADEMY	PACERS	WACO
PASADENA	EAGLES	PASADENA
PASCHAL	PANTHERS	FORT WORTH
PATTON SPRINGS	RANGERS	AFTON
PEARCE	MUSTANGS	RICHARDSON
PEARLAND	OILERS	PEARLAND
PEARSALL	MAVERICKS	PEARSALL

SCHOOL	MASCOT	CITY
PEASTER	GREYHOUNDS	PEASTER
PECOS	EAGLES	PECOS
PENELOPE	WOLVERINES	PENELOPE
PERMIAN	PANTHERS	ODESSA
PERRIN-WHITT	PIRATES	PERRIN
PERRYTON	RANGERS	PERRYTON
PETERSBURG	BUFFALOES	PETERSBURG
PETROLIA	PIRATES	PETROLIA
PETTUS	EAGLES	PETTUS
PEWITT	BRAHMAS	OMAHA
PFLUGERVILLE	PANTHERS	PFLUGERVILLE
PILOT POINT	BEARCATS	PILOT POINT
PINE DRIVE CHRISTIAN	EAGLES	DICKINSON
PINE TREE	PIRATES	LONGVIEW
PINKSTON	VIKINGS	DALLAS
PITTSBURG	PIRATES	PITTSBURG
PLAINS	COWBOYS	PLAINS
PLAINVIEW	BULLDOGS	PLAINVIEW
PLAINVIEW CHRISTIAN	EAGLES	PLAINVIEW
PLANO	WILDCATS	PLANO
PLANO EAST	PANTHERS	PLANO
PLANO WEST	WOLVES	PLANO
PLEASANT GROVE	HAWKS	PLEASANT GROVE
PLEASANTON	EAGLES	PLEASANTON
POLYTECHNIC	PARROTS	FORT WORTH
PONDER	LIONS	PONDER
POOLVILLE	MONARCHS	POOLVILLE
POPE JOHN XXIII	LIONS	KATY
PORT ARANSAS	MARLINS	PORT ARANSAS
PORT ISABEL	TARPONS	PORT ISABEL
PORT NECHES-GROVES	INDIANS	PORT NECHES-
PORTER, GLADYS	COWBOYS, FIGHTING	BROWNSVILLE
POST	ANTELOPES	POST
POTEET	PIRATES	MESQUITE
POTEET	AGGIES	POTEET
POTH	PIRATES	POTH
POTTSBORO	CARDINALS	POTTSBORO
PRAIRIE LEA	INDIANS	PRAIRIE LEA
PRAIRIE VALLEY	BULLDOGS	NOCONA
PRAIRILAND	PATRIOTS	PATTONVILLE
PREMONT	COWBOYS	PREMONT
PRESBYTERIAN PAN AMERICAN	EAGLES	KINGSVILLE
PRESIDIO	DEVILS, BLUE	PRESIDIO
PRESTONWOOD CHRISTIAN	LIONS	PLANO
PRIDDY	PIRATES	PRIDDY
PRINCE OF PEACE ACADEMY	EAGLES	CARROLTON
PRINCETON	PANTHERS	PRINCETON
PROGRESO	RED ANTS	PROGRESO

SCHOOL	MASCOT	CITY
PROSPER	EAGLES	PROSPER
PROVIDENCE	PROVETS	SAN ANTONIO
PROVIDENCE CLASSICAL	PALADINS	SPRING
P-SJ-A NORTH	RAIDERS	PHARR
P-SJ-A SOUTH	BEARS	SAN JUAN
QUANAH	INDIANS	QUANAH
QUEEN CITY	BULLDOGS	QUEEN CITY
QUITMAN	BULLDOGS	QUITMAN
RADFORD	KNIGHTS	EL PASO
RAINBOW HILLS BAPTIST	RAMS	SAN ANTONIO
RAINS	WILDCATS	RAINS
RALLS	JACKRABBITS	RALLS
RANCHVIEW	WOLVES	IRVING
RANDALL	RAIDERS	AMARILLO (CANYON ISD)
RANDOLPH	RO-HAWKS	UNIVERSAL CITY
RANGER	BULLDOGS	RANGER
RANKIN	DEVILS, RED	RANKIN
RAY	TEXANS, FIGHTING	CORPUS CHRISTI
RAYBURN, SAM	REBELS	IVANHOE
RAYBURN, SAM	TEXANS	PASADENA
RAYMONDVILLE	BEARCATS	RAYMONDVILLE
REAGAN COUNTY	OWLS	BIG LAKE
REAGAN, JH	BULLDOGS	HOUSTON
REAGAN, JH	RAIDERS	AUSTIN
REAGAN, R	RATTLERS	SAN ANTONIO
RED OAK	HAWKS	RED OAK
REDWATER	DRAGONS	REDWATER
REFUGIO	BOBCATS	REFUGIO
REGENTS SCHOOL	KNIGHTS	AUSTIN
REICHER CATHOLIC	COUGARS	WACO
RICE	BULLDOGS	RICE
RICE CONSOLIDATED	RAIDERS	ALTAIR
RICHARDS	PANTHERS	RICHARDS
RICHARDSON	EAGLES	RICHARDSON
RICHLAND	REBELS	NORTH RICHLAND HILLS
RICHLAND SPRINGS	COYOTES	RICHLAND SPRINGS
RIDER	RAIDERS	WICHITA FALLS
RIDGEWOOD CHRISTIAN	LIONS	PORT ARTHUR
RIESEL	INDIANS	RIESEL
RIO GRANDE CITY	RATTLERS	RIO GRANDE CITY
RIO HONDO	BOBCATS	RIO HONDO
RIO VISTA	EAGLES	RIO VISTA
RISING STAR	WILDCATS	RISING STAR

SCHOOL	MASCOT	CITY
RIVER ROAD	WILDCATS	AMARILLO
RIVERA	RAIDERS	BROWNSVILLE
RIVERCREST	REBELS	BOGOTA
RIVERSIDE	RANGERS	EL PASO
RIVIERA-KAUFER	SEAHAWKS	RIVIERA
ROBERT LEE	STEERS	ROBERT LEE
ROBINSON	ROCKETS	ROBINSON
ROBSTOWN	COTTONPICKERS	ROBSTOWN
ROBY	LIONS	ROBY
ROCHELLE	HORNETS	ROCHELLE
ROCKDALE	TIGERS	ROCKDALE
ROCKPORT-FULTON	PIRATES	ROCKPORT
ROCKSPRINGS	ANGORAS	ROCKSPRINGS
ROCKWALL	YELLOWJACKETS	ROCKWALL
ROCKWALL CHRISTIAN	WARRIORS	ROWLETT
ROGERS	EAGLES	ROGERS
ROMA	GLADIATORS	ROMA
ROOSEVELT	EAGLES	LUBBOCK
ROOSEVELT, FD	MUSTANGS	DALLAS
ROOSEVELT, T	ROUGH RIDERS	SAN ANTONIO
ROPES	EAGLES	ROPESVILLE
ROSCOE	PLOWBOYS	ROSCOE
ROSEBUD-LOTT	COUGARS	ROSEBUD
ROSEHILL CHRISTIAN	EAGLES	TOMBALL
ROTAN	YELLOWHAMMERS	ROTAN
ROUND ROCK	DRAGONS	ROUND ROCK
ROUND ROCK CHRISTIAN ACADEMY	CRUSADERS	ROUND ROCK
ROUNDTOP CARMINE	CUBS	CARMINE
ROWE	WARRIORS	McALLEN
ROWLETT	EAGLES	GARLAND
ROXTON	LIONS	ROXTON
ROYAL	FALCONS	BROOKSHIRE
ROYSE CITY	BULLDOGS	ROYSE CITY
RULE	BOBCATS	RULE
RUNGE	YELLOWJACKETS	RUNGE
RUSK	EAGLES	RUSK

Big Lake
Reagan County
Owls

Vanderbuilt
Industrial
Cobras

Pleasant Grove
Hawks

Caddo Mills
Foxes

SCHOOL	MASCOT	CITY
RYAN	RAIDERS	DENTON
RYLIE ACADEMY	KNIGHTS	DALLAS
S&S CONSOLIDATED	RAMS	SADLER
SABINAL	YELLOWJACKETS	SABINAL
SABINE	CARDINALS	GLADEWATER
SABINE PASS	SHARKS	SABINE PASS
SACHSE	MUSTANGS	SACHSE
SACRED HEART	INDIANS	HALLETSVILLE
SACRED HEART	TIGERS	MUENSTER
SAGINAW	ROUGH RIDERS	SAGINAW
SALADO	EAGLES	SALADO
SALTILLO	LIONS	SALTILLO
SAMNORWOOD	EAGLES	SAMNORWOOD
SAMUELL	SPARTANS	DALLAS
SAN ANGELO CENTRAL	BOBCATS	SAN ANGELO
SAN ANTONIO CHRISTIAN	LIONS	SAN ANTONIO
SAN AUGUSTINE	WOLVES	SAN AUGUSTINE
SAN BENITO	GREYHOUNDS	SAN BENITO
SAN DIEGO	VAQUEROS	SAN DIEGO
SAN ELIZARIO	EAGLES	SAN ELIZARIO
SAN ISIDRO	TIGERS	SAN ISIDRO
SAN JACINTO	COUGARS	BAYTOWN
SAN JACINTO CHRISTIAN ACADEMY	PATRIOTS	AMARILLO
SAN JUAN DIEGO CATHOLIC	SAINTS	AUSTIN
SAN MARCOS	RATTLERS	SAN MARCOS
SAN MARCOS BAPTIST	BEARS	SAN MARCOS
SAN PERLITA	TROJANS	SAN PERLITA
SAN SABA	ARMADILLOS	SAN SABA
SANDERSON	EAGLES	SANDERSON
SANDS	MUSTANGS	ACKERLY
SANFORD-FRITCH	EAGLES	FRITCH
SANGER	INDIANS	SANGER
SANTA ANNA	MOUNTAINEERS	SANTA ANNA
SANTA FE	INDIANS	SANTA FE
SANTA MARIA	COUGARS	SANTA MARIA
SANTA ROSA	WARRIORS	SANTA ROSA
SANTO	WILDCATS	SANTO
SAVOY	CARDINALS	SAVOY
SCARBOROUGH	SPARTANS	HOUSTON
SCHOOL OF EXCELLENCE	WOLVES	SAN ANTONIO
SCHULENBERG	SHORTHORNS	SCHULENBERG
SCIENCE & ENGINEERING, MAGNET SCHOOL	EAGLES	DALLAS
SCURRY-ROSSER	WILDCATS	SCURRY
SEAGOVILLE	DRAGONS	DALLAS
SEAGRAVES	EAGLES	SEAGRAVES
SEALY	TIGERS	SEALY
SECOND BAPTIST	EAGLES	HOUSTON

SCHOOL	MASCOT	CITY
SEGUIN	MATADORS	SEGUIN
SEGUIN, JUAN	COUGARS	ARLINGTON
SELWYN SCHOOL	UNICORNS	DENTON
SEMINOLE	INDIANS	SEMINOLE
SENDERO CHRISTIAN	MUSTANGS	SAN ANTONIO
SEVEN LAKES	SPARTANS	KATY
SEYMOUR	PANTHERS	SEYMOUR
SHADY GROVE CHRISTIAN	SAINTS	GRAND PRAIRIE
SHALLOWATER	MUSTANGS	SHALLOWATER
SHAMROCK	IRISH, FIGHTING	SHAMROCK
SHARPSTOWN	APOLLOS	HOUSTON
SHARYLAND	RATTLERS	MISSION
SHELBYVILLE	DRAGONS	SHELBYVILLE
SHELTON	CHARGERS	DALLAS
SHEPHERD	PIRATES	SHEPHERD
SHERMAN	BEARCATS	SHERMAN
SHINER	COMANCHES	SHINER
SHIPTON	STALLIONS	PLANO
SHOEMAKER	WOLVES, GREY	KILLEEN
SIDNEY	EAGLES	SIDNEY
SIERRA BLANCA	VAQUEROS	SIERRA BLANCA
SILSBEE	TIGERS	SILSBEE
SILVERTON	OWLS	SILVERTON
SINTON	PIRATES	SINTON
SKIDMORE-TYNAN	BOBCATS	SKIDMORE
SKYLINE	RAIDERS	DALLAS
SLATON	TIGERS	SLATON
SLIDELL	GREYHOUNDS	SLIDELL
SLOCUM	MUSTANGS	SLOCUM
SMILEY	EAGLES, GOLDEN	HOUSTON
SMITH, A MACEO	FALCONS	DALLAS
SMITH, NEWMAN	TROJANS	CARROLLTON
SMITHSON VALLEY	RANGERS	SPRING BRANCH
SMITHVILLE	TIGERS	SMITHVILLE
SMYER	BOBCATS	SMYER
SNOOK	BLUEJAYS	SNOOK
SNYDER	TIGERS	SNYDER
SOCORRO	BULLDOGS	EL PASO
SOMERSET	BULLDOGS	SOMERSET
SOMERVILLE	YEGUAS	SOMERVILLE
SONORA	BRONCOS	SONORA
SONRISE CHRISTIAN	CHRISTIAN SUNS	SAN ANTONIO
SOUTH GARLAND	COLONELS	GARLAND
SOUTH GRAND PRAIRIE	WARRIORS	GRAND PRAIRIE
SOUTH HILLS	SCORPIONS	FORT WORTH
SOUTH HOUSTON	TROJANS	HOUSTON
SOUTH OAK CLIFF	BEARS, GOLDEN	DALLAS
SOUTH SAN ANTONIO	BOBCATS	SAN ANTONIO

SCHOOL	MASCOT	CITY
SOUTH SAN ANTONIO WEST	COUGARS, FIGHTING	SAN ANTONIO
SOUTH SHAVER BAPTIST	EAGLES, FIGHTING	HOUSTON
SOUTHEAST ACADEMY	FALCONS	HOUSTON
SOUTHLAND	EAGLES	SOUTHLAND
SOUTHSHORE CHRISTIAN ACADEMY	STINGRAYS	LEAGUE CITY
SOUTHSIDE	CARDINALS	SAN ANTONIO
SOUTHWEST	DRAGONS	SAN ANTONIO
SOUTHWEST	RAIDERS	FORT WORTH
SOUTHWEST CHRISTIAN	EAGLES	FORT WORTH
SOUTHWEST CHRISTIAN	SAINTS	HOUSTON
SPADE	LONGHORNS	SPADE
SPEARMAN	LYNX	SPEARMAN
SPLENDORA	WILDCATS	SPLENDORA
SPRING	LIONS	SPRING
SPRING HILL	PANTHERS	LONGVIEW
SPRING WOODS	TIGERS	HOUSTON
SPRINGLAKE-EARTH	WOLVERINES	EARTH
SPRINGTOWN	PORCUPINES	SPRINGTOWN
SPRUCE	TIMBERWOLVES	DALLAS
SPUR	BULLDOGS	SPUR
SPURGER	PIRATES	SPURGER
ST AGNES	TIGERS	HOUSTON
ST ALBANS	CENTURIONS	ARLINGTON
ST ANDREWS EPISCOPAL	CRUSADERS	AUSTIN
ST ANTHONY CATHOLIC	YELLOWJACKETS	SAN ANTONIO
ST AUGUSTINE	KNIGHTS	LAREDO
ST FRANCIS GIRLS ACADEMY	SKYLARKS	SAN ANTONIO
ST GERARD	ROYALS	SAN ANTONIO
ST JO	PANTHERS	ST JO
ST JOHNS	CRUSADERS	ENNIS
ST JOHNS	REBELS	HOUSTON
ST JOSEPH	EAGLES	BRYAN
ST JOSEPH	FLYERS	VICTORIA
ST JOSEPH ACADEMY	BLOODHOUNDS	BROWNSVILLE
ST MARKS SCHOOL OF TEXAS	LIONS	DALLAS
ST MARYS HALL	BARONS	SAN ANTONIO
ST MICHAEL ACADEMY	DRAGON SLAYERS	BRYAN

Plano West
Wolves

El Campo
Ricebirds

Brownsville
Livingway Christian
Warriors

Athens
Yellowjackets

174

SCHOOL	MASCOT	CITY
ST MICHAELS ACADEMY	CRUSADERS	AUSTIN
ST PAUL	CARDINALS	SHINER
ST PIUS X	PANTHERS	HOUSTON
ST STEPHENS EPISCOPAL	BULLDOGS	HOUSTON
ST STEPHENS EPISCOPAL	SPARTANS	AUSTIN
ST THOMAS	EAGLES	HOUSTON
ST THOMAS EPISCOPAL	SAINTS	HOUSTON
STACY	EAGLES	SAN ANTONIO
STAFFORD	SPARTANS	STAFFORD
STAMFORD	BULLDOGS	STAMFORD
STANTON	BUFFALOES	STANTON
STAR	TIGERS	STAR
STEELE	KNIGHTS	SCHERTZ
STEPHENVILLE	YELLOWJACKETS	STEPHENVILLE
STERLING	RAIDERS	HOUSTON
STERLING	RANGERS	BAYTOWN
STERLING CITY	EAGLES	STERLING CITY
STOCKDALE	BRAHMAS	STOCKDALE
STONY POINT	TIGERS	ROUND ROCK
STRAKE JESUIT	CRUSADERS	HOUSTON
STRATFORD	SPARTANS	HOUSTON
STRATFORD	ELKS	STRATFORD
STRAWN	GREYHOUNDS	STRAWN
SUCCESS HIGH SCHOOL	OWLS	FORT WORTH
SUDAN	HORNETS	SUDAN
SULPHUR BLUFF	BEARS	SULPHUR BLUFF
SULPHUR SPRINGS	WILDCATS	SULPHUR SPRINGS
SUMMIT	JAGUARS	ARLINGTON
SUMMIT	TIGERS	MANSFIELD
SUMMIT CHRISTIAN	EAGLES	CEDAR PARK
SUNDOWN	ROUGHNECKS	SUNDOWN
SUNNYBROOK CHRISTIAN	LIONS	SAN ANTONIO
SUNRAY	BOBCATS	SUNRAY
SUNSET	BISON	DALLAS
SWEENY	BULLDOGS	SWEENY
SWEETWATER	MUSTANGS	SWEETWATER
SWEETWATER CHRISTIAN	CRUSADERS	HOUSTON
TAFT	GREYHOUNDS	TAFT
TAFT, WM H	RAIDERS	SAN ANTONIO
TAHOKA	BULLDOGS	TAHOKA
TALENTED AND GIFTED, MAGNET SCHOOL FOR	GRIFFIN	DALLAS
TARKINGTON	LONGHORNS	CLEVELAND
TASCOSA	REBELS	AMARILLO
TATUM	EAGLES	TATUM
TAYLOR	DUCKS	TAYLOR
TAYLOR	LIONS	ALIEF
TAYLOR, JAMES	MUSTANGS	KATY

SCHOOL	MASCOT	CITY
TEAGUE	LIONS	TEAGUE
TEMPLE	WILDCATS	TEMPLE
TEMPLE CHRISTIAN	BLAZERS	DALLAS
TEMPLE CHRISTIAN	EAGLES	FORT WORTH
TEMPLE CHRISTIAN	WATCHMEN	LEWISVILLE
TENAHA	TIGERS	TENAHA
TERRELL	TIGERS	TERRELL
TERRELL CHRISTIAN ACADEMY	EAGLES	TERRELL
TERRY	RANGERS	ROSENBURG
TEXAS	TIGERS	TEXARKANA
TEXAS CHRISTIAN	LIGHTS	HOUSTON
TEXAS CHRISTIAN	STARS	WACO
TEXAS CHRISTIAN ACADEMY	SPARTANS	ARLINGTON
TEXAS CITY	STINGAREES	TEXAS CITY
TEXAS MILITARY INSTITUTE	PANTHERS	SAN ANTONIO
TEXAS SCHOOL FOR THE BLIND	WILDCATS	AUSTIN
TEXAS SCHOOL FOR THE DEAF	RANGERS	AUSTIN
TEXLINE	TORNADOES	TEXLINE
TEXOMA CHRISTIAN	EAGLES	SHERMAN
THE BANFF SCHOOL	BEARS	HOUSTON
THE COLONY	COUGARS	THE COLONY
THE WOODLANDS	HIGHLANDERS	THE WOODLANDS
THE WOODLANDS - COLLEGE PARK	CAVALIERS	THE WOODLANDS
THE WOODLANDS - McMULLOUGH CAMPUS	HIGHLANDERS	THE WOODLANDS
THORNDALE	BULLDOGS	THORNDALE
THRALL	TIGERS	THRALL
THREE RIVERS	BULLDOGS	THREE RIVERS
THREE WAY	EAGLES	MAPLE
THROCKMORTON	GREYHOUNDS	THROCKMORTON
TIDEHAVEN	TIGERS	EL MATON
TIMBERVIEW	WOLVES	MANSFIELD
TIMPSON	BEARS	TIMPSON
TIVY	ANTLERS	KERRVILLE
TOLAR	RATTLERS	TOLAR
TOM BEAN	TOMCATS	TOM BEAN
TOMBALL	COUGARS	TOMBALL
TORNILLO	COYOTES	TORNILLO
TOWN EAST	EAGLES	SAN ANTONIO
TRAVIS	REBELS	AUSTIN
TRENT	GORILLAS	TRENT
TRENTON	TIGERS	TRENTON
TRIMBLE TECH	BULLDOGS	FORT WORTH
TRINIDAD	TROJANS	TRINIDAD
TRINITY	TIGERS	TRINITY
TRINITY	CHARGERS	MIDLAND
TRINITY	TROJANS	EULESS
TRINITY CHRISTIAN	EAGLES	ALEDO
TRINITY CHRISTIAN	EAGLES	SAN ANTONIO

SCHOOL	MASCOT	CITY
TRINITY CHRISTIAN	LIONS	LUBBOCK
TRINITY CHRISTIAN	TIGERS	CEDAR HILL
TRINITY CHRISTIAN ACADEMY	TROJANS	ADDISON
TRINITY FELLOWSHIP	LIONS	AMARILLO
TRINITY SCHOOL OF TEXAS	TITANS	LONGVIEW
TRINITY VALLEY	TROJANS	FORT WORTH
TRIUMPH CHRISTIAN	BULLDOGS	PORTER
TROUP	TIGERS	TROUP
TROY	TROJANS	TROY
TULIA	HORNETS	TULIA
TULOSO-MIDWAY	WARRIORS	CORPUS CHRISTI
TURNER	LIONS	CARROLLTON
TWIN LAKES CHRISTIAN	TRAILBLAZERS	CEDAR PARK
TYLER ST CHRISTIAN	CRUSADERS	DALLAS
TYLER, JOHN	LIONS	TYLER
UNION GROVE	LIONS	GLADEWATER
UNION HILL	BULLDOGS	GILMER
UNITED	LONGHORNS	LAREDO
UNITED SOUTH	PANTHERS	LAREDO
UNIVERSAL ACADEMY	EAGLES	IRVING
UNIVERSITY	TROJANS	WACO
UNIVERSITY PREP SCHOOL	OWLS	HARLINGEN
URSULINE ACADEMY	BEARS	DALLAS
UTOPIA	BUFFALOES	UTOPIA
UVALDE	COYOTES	UVALDE
VALENTINE	PIRATES	VALENTINE
VALLEY	PATRIOTS	TURKEY
VALLEY CHRISTIAN SCHOOL	CHAPARRALS	MISSION
VALLEY MILLS	EAGLES	VALLEY MILLS
VALLEY VIEW	TIGERS	PHARR
VAN	VANDALS	VAN
VAN ALSTYNE	PANTHERS	VAN ALSTYNE
VAN HORN	EAGLES	VAN HORN
VAN VLECK	LEOPARDS	VAN VLECK
VANGUARD	VIKINGS	WACO
VANGUARD CHRISTIAN	KNIGHTS	BOERNE
VEGA	LONGHORNS	VEGA
VENUS	BULLDOGS	VENUS
VERNON	LIONS	VERNON
VETERANS MEMORIAL	PATRIOTS	MISSION
VICTORY CHRISTIAN	COUGARS	BASTROP
VICTORY CHRISTIAN	EAGLES	LANCASTER
VIDOR	PIRATES	VIDOR
VINES	VIKINGS	PLANO
VISTA RIDGE	RANGERS	CEDAR PARK

177

SCHOOL	MASCOT	CITY
WACO	LIONS	WACO
WACO CHRISTIAN FELLOWSHIP	SAINTS	WACO
WACO CHRISTIAN FELLOWSHIP	WARRIORS	WACO
WAELDER	WILDCATS	WAELDER
WAGNER	THUNDERBIRDS	JUDSON
WALDORF SCHOOL	ROADRUNNERS	AUSTIN
WALL	HAWKS	WALL
WALLER	BULLDOGS	WALLER
WALNUT SPRINGS	HORNETS	WALNUT SPRINGS
WALTRIP	RAMS	HOUSTON
WARREN	WARRIORS	SAN ANTONIO
WARREN	WARRIORS	WARREN
WASHINGTON, BT	EAGLES	HOUSTON
WASHINGTON, BT, MAGNET, PERFORMING ARTS	PEGASUS	DALLAS
WASKOM	WILDCATS	WASKOM
WATER VALLEY	WILDCATS	WATER VALLEY
WAXAHACHIE	INDIANS	WAXAHACHIE
WEATHERFORD	KANGAROOS	WEATHERFORD
WEIMAR	WILDCATS	WEIMAR
WELLINGTON	SKYROCKETS	WELLINGTON
WELLMAN UNION	WILDCATS	WELLMAN
WELLS	PIRATES	WELLS
WESLACO	PANTHERS	WESLACO
WESLACO EAST	WILDCATS	WESLACO
WEST	TROJANS	WEST
WEST HARDIN	OILERS	SARATOGA
WEST HOUSTON CHRISTIAN SCHOOL	KNIGHTS	HOUSTON
WEST MESQUITE	WRANGLERS	MESQUITE
WEST ORANGE-STARK	MUSTANGS	ORANGE
WEST OSO	BEARS	CORPUS CHRISTI
WEST RUSK	RAIDERS	NEW LONDON
WEST SABINE	TIGERS	PINELAND
WEST SIDE MONASTERY	ROYALS	HOUSTON
WEST TEXAS	COMANCHES	STINNETT
WEST BROOK	BRUINS	BEAUMONT
WESTBROOK	WILDCATS	WESTBROOK
WESTBURY	REBELS, ROWDY	HOUSTON

Boerne
Greyhounds

Azle
Hornets

Lubbock Estacado
Matadors

Houston Strake
Jesuit Crusaders

SCHOOL	MASCOT	CITY
WESTBURY CHRISTIAN	WILDCATS	HOUSTON
WESTERN HILLS	COUGARS	FORT WORTH
WESTFIELD	MUSTANGS	HOUSTON
WESTLAKE	CHAPARRALS	AUSTIN
WESTSIDE	WOLVES	HOUSTON
WESTWOOD	PANTHERS	PALESTINE
WESTWOOD	WARRIORS	AUSTIN
WHARTON	TIGERS	WHARTON
WHEATLEY, P	WILDCATS	HOUSTON
WHEELER	MUSTANGS	WHEELER
WHITE DEER	BUCKS	WHITE DEER
WHITE OAK	ROUGHNECKS	WHITE OAK
WHITE,WT	LONGHORNS	DALLAS
WHITEFACE	ANTELOPES	WHITEFACE
WHITEHOUSE	WILDCATS	WHITEHOUSE
WHITESBORO	BEARCATS	WHITESBORO
WHITEWRIGHT	TIGERS	WHITEWRIGHT
WHITHARRAL	PANTHERS	WHITHARRAL
WHITNEY	WILDCATS	WHITNEY
WICHITA CHRISTIAN	STARS	WICHITA FALLS
WICHITA FALLS	COYOTES	WICHITA FALLS
WILLIAMS	WARRIORS	PLANO
WILLIS	WILDKATS	WILLIS
WILLOWRIDGE	EAGLES	SUGARLAND
WILLS POINT	TIGERS	WILLS POINT
WILSON	MUSTANGS	WILSON
WILSON, WOODROW	WILDCATS	DALLAS
WIMBERLEY	TEXANS	WIMBERLEY
WINDTHORST	TROJANS	WINDTHORST
WINK	WILDCATS	WINK
WINNSBORO	RAIDERS, RED	WINNSBORO
WINONA	WILDCATS	WINONA
WINSTON	EAGLES	SAN ANTONIO
WINSTON	EAGLES	SAN ANTONIO
WINTERS	BLIZZARDS	WINTERS
WODEN	EAGLES	WODEN
WOLFE CITY	WOLVES	WOLFE CITY
WOODLANDS CHRISTIAN	WARRIORS	CONROE
WOODSBORO	EAGLES	WOODSBORO
WOODSON	COWBOYS	WOODSON
WOODVILLE	EAGLES	WOODVILLE
WORTHAM	BULLDOGS	WORTHAM
WORTHING	COLTS	HOUSTON
WYATT, OD	CHAPARRALS	FORT WORTH
WYLIE	BULLDOGS	ABILENE
WYLIE	PIRATES	WYLIE

SCHOOL	MASCOT	CITY
YANTIS	OWLS	YANTIS
YATES	LIONS	HOUSTON
YES COLLEGE PREP	WIZARDS	HOUSTON
YOAKUM	BULLDOGS	YOAKUM
YOE	YOEMEN	CAMERON
YORKTOWN	WILDCATS	YORKTOWN
YSLETA	INDIANS	EL PASO
ZAPATA	HAWKS	ZAPATA
ZAVALLA	EAGLES	ZAVALLA
ZEPHYR	BULLDOGS	ZEPHYR

Appendix C
Mascot-Related School Addresses by the Numbers

1   Trojan Drive—Charlotte

1   Greyhound Lane—Boerne

1   Coyote Trail—Alice

1   Coyote Trail—Uvalde

1   Longhorn Boulevard—Cedar Hill

1   Bulldog Drive—Everman

1   Bulldog Drive—Jefferson of Jefferson

1   Eagle Drive—Bruceville-Eddy of Eddy

1   Eagle Drive—Jonesboro

1   Yellowjacket Road—Kemp

1   Lion Avenue—Livingston

1   Lion Country Drive—Lockhart

1   Lion Drive—New Boston

1   Raider Circle—Northbrook of Houston

1   Wildcat Drive—Big Sandy of Big Sandy

1   Bobcat Trail—Gary

1   Bearcat Drive—Whitesboro

1   Bearkat Boulevard—Raymondville

1   Tiger Avenue—Wharton

1   Battlin' Buc Boulevard—Corpus Christi Miller

88   Jaguar Drive—Central of Beaumont

100   Bulldog Drive—Jasper

100   Shark Avenue—Palacios

100   Wildcat Drive—Kirbyville

100   East Jersey Drive—Falfurrias

100-A	Elk Drive—Burleson
111	East Harvester—Pampa
200	Pirate Drive—Crawford
200	Tiger Drive—Daingerfield
203	Seahawk Drive—Riviera-Kaufer of Riviera
300	Eagle Lane—Prosper
300	Warrior Trail—South Grand Prairie
321	Panther Parkway—Princeton
400	Eagleland Drive—Brackenridge of San Antonio
400	North Pirate Boulevard—Sinton
500	Lobo Lane—Little Elm
600	Eagle Drive—De Soto
600	Colonel Drive—South Garland
600	Mustang Avenue—Denver City
604	North Coyote Boulevard—La Joya
701	North Cub—Brownfield
705	Rabbit Boulevard—Atlanta
708	Tiger Drive—Belton
939	West Tiger Lane—Sealy
1000	Lumberjack Drive—Diboll
1002	Warpath—Bonham
1002	Texan Trail—Ray of Corpus Christi
1100	Pickerlane Drive—Robstown
1500	Lone Wolf Blvd.—Colorado City
1900	Maverick Drive—Marshall
1990	Maverick Drive—Pearsall
2101	Mustang Drive—Marble Falls
2201	Brahma Boulevard—King of Kingsville
2301	Texan Drive—Northwest of Justin
2807	Mustang Drive—Ingleside
2905	Leopard Drive—Liberty-Eylau of Texarkana
3223	Mustang Drive—Grapevine
3333	Hurricane Lane—Hightower of Missouri City

3801   Ram Boulevard—Mineral Wells
4001   Wildcat Lane—Calallen of Corpus Christi
4601   Wildcat Drive—Gregory-Portland
4606   Mustang Avenue—Lamar of Rosenberg
5202   Bear Lane—West Oso of Corpus Christi
5506   Bulldog Drive—Marion

11914 Dragon Lane—Southwest of San Antonio

Others

El Paso Coronado	100 Champions Place
Arlington Houston	2000 Sam Houston Road
Grand Prairie	101 High School Drive
Johnson City LBJ	303 North LBJ Drive
Seguin Lifegate Christian	395 Lifegate Lane
San Antonio Memorial	1227 Memorial
The Woodlands John Cooper	1 John Cooper Drive
Fort Worth Country Day School	4200 Country Day Lane
Dawson of Dawson	199 North School Avenue
Houston Kinkaid	201 Kinkaid Road
San Antonio Ronald Reagan	19000 Ronald Reagan
Red Oak	154 Louise Ritter Boulevard

(Ritter, a Red Oak grad, was the surprise gold medalist in the woman's high jump in the 1988 Olympics.)

Brownsville St. Joseph	101 St. Joseph Drive
Bridgeport	1 Maroon Drive
Mesquite Poteet	3300 Poteet Drive

Dallas Hillcrest, however, is named for the street, not vice versa.

And without numbers

Calhoun of Port Lavaca	Sandcrab Boulevard
Harker Heights	Knights Way
Hico	Tiger Road

Acknowledgments

The most important written source for this work was *2004-2005 Texas Sports Guide of High Schools and Colleges,* a work published annually for coaches and schools in the state. It includes vital statistics for the schools, names the coaches in each sport, lists telephone numbers, and, most importantly for us, indicates the names of the mascots. A more specialized book was also useful— *Texas High School Hotshots: The Stars before They Were Stars* by Alan Burton.

In this day and age, internet websites are important sources of information, even if they have to be used with more caution than published materials. Most Texas high schools have such sites and they are very helpful, though sometimes difficult to mine. Likewise, famous persons frequently have official and unofficial web pages that occasionally address their high school origins. The most useful general website for mascots was www.texasmascots.com hosted by Kent Gilley. Another important source was www.tapps.net, the site for the Texas Association of Private and Parochial Schools.

But most of the material in the book came from the schools themselves (a) in the form of answers to a questionnaire sent to a sample of schools in the state or (b) from telephone interviews with representatives of the districts. Without the kindness of these folks in responding to our requests, the book would have been seriously deficient in the stories of where the mascots came from and what they mean. We cannot list the names of these sources, but we are grateful to each one.

Over the years, numerous articles, often tongue-in-cheek, have discussed the mascot phenomenon. These appeared in national news magazines and sports magazines or in newspaper columns devoted to features and to sports. Some compile lists of the most unusual names. Many others play "the mascot game" by suggesting more appropriate or more humorous team names. We have tried to resist that temptation, though with only partial success.

The author expresses his thanks particularly to the late Richard Dillard (a Panther), with whom the project was first shared in the 1980s; Glenn Dromgoole (a Warrior), editor of State House Press, and his assistant Carly Kahl (a Mustang) for decisions on concept and for information; to the Grady McWhiney Foundation, for whom the author is Historian-in-Residence; and to other friends and relations who shared ideas and critiques.